DATE DUE

MR 1 7 '95			
DE 8 '95			
Mar 14			

DEMCO 38-296

Implementing Family-Centered Services in Early Intervention:
A Team-Based Model for Change

Donald B. Bailey, Jr.
P. J. McWilliam
Pamela J. Winton
Rune J. Simeonsson

Carolina Institute for Research on
Infant Personnel Preparation

BROOKLINE
BOOKS

PO Box 1046
Cambridge, MA 02238

Frank Porter Graham Child Development Center
University of North Carolina at Chapel Hill

Published by

Brookline Books

P.O. Box 1046, Cambridge, MA 02238-1046
Order also by telephone: 617-868-0360
and by FAX: 617-868-1772

Table of Contents

SECTION II: Guidelines and Materials for Conducting the Workshop

SECTION III: Appendices

Preface

WHAT DOES IT MEAN TO BE FAMILY-CENTERED when working with infants and preschoolers with disabilities? The requirement of Public Law 99-457 for an Individualized Family Service Plan is one of many forces redirecting early intervention efforts to include a focus on the family. Although the philosophical notion of family support is generally well-accepted among professionals, changing current practices and priorities will likely be difficult.

This monograph describes a team-based decision-making workshop for implementing family-centered services in early intervention. It differs from a "training" curriculum in that it focuses on the decisions that teams must make as they seek to become family-centered. The primary purpose of the workshop is to provide a structure for teams to (1) identify concrete dimensions of a family-centered approach, (2) assess the extent to which their program currently follows those practices, (3) identify and establish priorities for change, and (4) develop a plan for ensuring that change occurs. The model has evolved out of a wide range of experiences in working with professionals from various disciplines and many different types of programs.

The monograph contains two sections. Section I describes the background and basis for family-centered services in early intervention, identifies barriers to implementing a family focus, and presents a rationale and overview of the model. The primary components of the model are described and considerations in preparing for the activities are presented. Also, strategies for evaluating the effectiveness of the model are suggested. Section II provides goals for each component of the workshop and a suggested outline for activities related to six Key Questions about family-centered services. The activities consist of presentations, case study discussions, and small group decision-making tasks.

Handouts and master copies for overhead transparencies or slides are included for each set of activities and are to be found in Appendices D and E, respectively.

SECTION I:
Introduction and Overview

Chapter 1

Background and Rationale

THE IMPETUS FOR A FAMILY-CENTERED APPROACH to early intervention comes from two primary sources: federal legislation and current conceptualizations of best practice. This section describes these bases, identifies barriers to implementing a family focus, and presents an overall rationale and description of the model.

Public Law 99-457

Public Law 99-457 establishes a firm philosophical as well as functional basis for family-centered services in early intervention. Philosophically, the regulations emphasize the interrelationships between children and families and establish family support as a key goal for early intervention services:

> *Part H recognizes the unique and critical role that families play in the development of infants and toddlers who are eligible under this Part. It is clear, both from the statute and the legislative history of the Act, that the Congress intended for families to plan an active, collaborative role in the planning and provision of early intervention services. Thus, these regulations . . . should have a positive impact on the family, because they strengthen the authority and encourage the increased participation of parents in meeting the early intervention needs of their children. (Federal Register, June 22, 1989, 54, p. 26309)*

The comments accompanying the regulations emphasize the role of parents as decision makers in determining the extent to which they accept or decline services, and the importance of family choice, consent, and involvement is reflected throughout the regulations. Recent changes embedded in P. L. 102-119 (reauthorizing and amending Part H of P. L. 99-457) further reinforce the family aspects of early intervention and clarify regulations and procedures.

The requirement for an Individualized Family Service Plan (IFSP) is the most visible and often-discussed aspect of the legislation with respect to a family-centered approach. The IFSP must include, in addition to the child components required in the IEP, a documentation of family strengths and needs, a specification of major family outcomes, a description of services to be provided for the family, and the name of a service coordinator who is to assist the family in implementing the plan and coordinating services with other agencies and persons. Clearly, however, a family-centered approach is broader than the IFSP. Also, it is clear that the way the law is implemented will vary widely across states and communities, emphasizing the importance of local planning and decision-making.

Best Practices

The law and its regulations should be viewed in the broader context of shifting views about the purpose of early intervention and what is meant by best practice. Over the past five years, it has been argued that a primary mission for early intervention is to provide family support. According to Zigler and Black (1989), the ultimate goal of family support programs is to "enable families to be independent by developing their own informal support networks" (p. 11). In early intervention, numerous labels have been applied to the family support movement, including parent empowerment (Dunst, 1985; Dunst, Trivette, & Deal, 1988), family-focused intervention (Bailey, Simeonsson, Winton, Huntington, Comfort, Isbell, O'Donnell, & Helm, 1986), and family-centered care (Shelton, Jeppson, & Johnson, 1987). Although these models differ in some respects, each emphasizes (a) the importance of family support as a primary goal of early intervention, and (b) the expectation that families should be able to choose their level of involvement in program planning, decision-making, and service delivery. Brewer, McPherson, Magrab, and Hutchins (1989) describe family-centered care as follows:

> *Family-centered care is the focus of philosophy of care in which the pivotal role of the family is recognized and respected in the lives of children with special health needs. Within this philosophy is the idea that families should be supported in their natural care-giving and decision-making roles by building on their unique strengths as people and families. In this philosophy, patterns of living at home and in the community are promoted; parents and professionals are seen as equals in a partnership committed to the development of optimal quality in the delivery of all levels of health care. To achieve this, elements of family-centered care and community-based care must be carefully interwoven into a full and effective coordination of the care of all children with special health needs.*
>
> (p. 1055)

From a philosophical perspective, it is clear that a family-centered approach is not defined by the use of a particular form or by the provision of a specific type of service. Rather it is reflected in the willingness of an agency or program to develop a collaborative relationship with each individual family and to provide services in accordance with family values and priorities. Thus the model described in this monograph addresses the implementation of a family-centered approach through-out each major aspect of program services.

Potential Barriers to Implementing Family-centered Services

Despite the obvious importance of a family focus, its implementation has proven to be a challenging task, for a number of reasons. First, most teachers and allied health professionals enter their respective fields out of a desire to work with children and they receive training that is almost exclusively child-focused (Bailey, Simeonsson, Yoder, & Huntington, 1990). Thus many have neither the skills nor expectation to work with families. Second, a family-centered philosophy challenges the long-held view of the professional as the primary decision-maker in the management of young children with disabilities, since a fundamental tenet of the family support movement is family choice and a responsiveness to family priorities (Bailey, 1987). Relinquishing control of decisions about the nature and extent of early intervention services is likely to be viewed as threatening by many professionals. Third, professionals work in service delivery systems designed to provide child-based services. In a recent study, we found that systems barriers were mentioned by professionals as one of the major reasons why they were not more family-centered in their services (Bailey, Buysse, Edmondson, & Smith, 1992). Furthermore, we found that many professionals felt that families had neither the interest nor the skills needed to fully participate in program planning and decision-making. Finally, each of these factors is exacerbated by the uncertainty surrounding the actual implementation of a family-centered approach and the specific requirements to be followed. Many states have yet to develop guidelines for the IFSP or to provide comprehensive training for professionals with regard to either the guidelines or skills and procedures needed to implement the law (Harbin, Gallagher, & Lillie, 1989).

The Need for a New Model of Training

The combination of these factors—a major shift in roles and practices, a complex and varied requirement, and lack of training or administrative support—means that implementing a family-centered approach in early intervention is likely to be a difficult and long-term process. Our studies to date suggest that professionals do in fact perceive a need for change; they aspire to high levels of family-centered services and report a significant discrepancy between current and ideal practices (Bailey et al., 1992). When asked the reasons for this discrepancy, administrative and family factors are likely to be mentioned as barriers to change. Also, we have found that many professionals believe that they themselves do not have the authority to make such a change. A great deal of uncertainty exists as professionals wait for guidelines and decisions to be made at higher administrative levels.

The major purpose of this monograph is to provide a series of activities to help programs facilitate changes in the way early intervention services are provided, with the goal of creating a more family-centered endeavor. Several propositions about the change process have helped shape the nature and form of the activities described (Winton, 1990):

1. Change is always a difficult process. It is likely to be especially difficult when the change involves an orientation that differs substantially from current practices.

2. Change is a gradual process best facilitated by ongoing staff development activities.

3. When teams are involved in providing services, training must begin at the team level so that individuals within the organization develop a shared knowledge and value base.

4. A major goal of training should be to empower trainees to become independent and competent problem-solvers, capable of assessing and monitoring their own needs.

5. When possible and appropriate, consumers of services should be given opportunities to provide input to decisions about changes to be made.

These assumptions have led to the development of a model of training that addresses some of the major decisions that professionals need to make about their work with families. As described in the next chapter, this model is team-based in its focus, provides the necessary background information and structure to facilitate team decision-making activities, and includes parents as participants in the process. The training activities are designed to identify where teams are in their current practices and build on existing resources for change.

Chapter 2

Overview of Workshop Components

THE WORKSHOP FOR IMPLEMENTING A FAMILY-CENTERED APPROACH in early intervention programs contains seven key components: (1) team-based training, (2) parent participation, (3) a decision-oriented format, (4) guided decision-making activities, (5) goal-setting, (6) core reading assignments; and (7) effective leadership. In this section we provide a description and rationale for each component.

Team-Based Training

The primary target audience for this training is professionals working in early intervention programs serving infants and toddlers with disabilities and their families, although it would also be useful for any service program that wanted to be more family-centered. Most early intervention programs use a team approach involving professionals from diverse disciplines to provide comprehensive services. In addition, all programs have some sort of administrative or supervisory hierarchy. The way teams are configured and administered will vary considerably from program to program. Also, within teams there will often be considerable variability in individual commitment to family-centered services.

Two fundamental assumptions about early intervention programs and a family-centered approach are central to this model of training. The first is that providing support to families should be part of each professional's work. This means that each professional will need to ask how he or she can change practices in order to be more responsive to family needs and priorities. The second assumption is that moving to family-centered services must also be a decision that is made by the team as a whole. Without a shared commitment to families, services are likely to be fragmented and inconsistent. Families will get one message from some team members and another from others. Part of being family-centered is the provision of coordinated services based on a shared philosophy of how families are involved in every aspect of service delivery, whether it be assessment, child care, family support, therapeutic services, case management, team meetings, or consultation.

Some workshops are directed toward specific individuals for the purpose of teaching specific skills. Such an approach will not work, however, if the training involves issues which affect all team members in some way. The activities described in this monograph assume that all team members are present during the entire set of activities. Also assumed is that key administrators are there. Our research has clearly documented that professionals who actually provide services to children and families perceive substantial administrative barriers to implementing a family-centered approach. By participating in these activities, administrators send a message to service providers that they endorse the decision-making activities being conducted and that they are willing to work with professionals to change program practices. Such participation is essential, because teams often will make decisions as a result of these activities that will require administrative support. Also, by being present during the activities, administrators will gain a better understanding of the rationale behind the decisions made and can be a part of the decision-making process.

Our experiences indicate that getting all team members to commit time to activities such as those described here is difficult. Even more challenging is for administrators to find the time to attend and participate fully. We believe, however, that the sacrifices required will be worth it in the long run as services are implemented in a philosophically consistent fashion.

The number and type of teams included in any single workshop is variable. We recommend, however, that (a) the participants in the workshop serve a common or adjacent geographical areas, and (b) the total number of persons not exceed 50.

Finally, it is essential that key decision-makers in the agency or organization are aware of the nature of the activities being planned. Even if they cannot attend or participate in the training, every effort should be made to ensure that they know the kinds of questions being asked and the types of decisions that are likely to be made. Ultimately the successful implementation of those decisions will depend on their support. Also, if they can endorse the training and decision-making process (even though they do not know what the outcome will be), participants will feel that their time is being spent in a worthwhile fashion and that the decisions being made have a chance of being implemented.

Family Participation

One question that will need to be decided in planning to conduct the activities described is whether parents or other caregivers will be invited to participate. Several benefits of family participation are possible. Since families will be the primary recipients of a family-focused approach to services, it seems only logical that they should have input into how those services should be provided. Including families in the activities should increase the likelihood that the decisions made are acceptable to families. Family members can present a perspective that professionals cannot. Furthermore, including families in these activities is consistent with a family-centered philosophy and establishes a precedent for families serving in a role of decision-maker.

If families are included in the decision-making activities, several important points should be noted:

1. Professionals participating in the workshop should be involved in the decision to invite parents to participate.

2. Family members who participate should be able to participate in the same ways as the professionals.

3. The purpose of having family members present—that is, to assist teams in making decisions about program practices—should be clear to both family members and professionals.

4. Parents or other family members often have difficulty committing the time demanded by the activities. We have found that paying parents a consulting fee and helping with child care greatly increases the likelihood of full participation.

5. The role of the leader in encouraging family participation and responding to comments made by family members is essential.

6. Our experiences suggest that success in family participation is likely to be greatest when the family members invited to participate are those who:

   a. currently have children being served by the team;
   b. have been in the program for at least one year; and
   c. can serve as representatives of the broad array of families served by the program.

A Decision-Oriented Format

In many ways the experiences described here should not be referred to as "training" activities. A more accurate portrayal would be that they are activities designed to assist teams in a process of self-examination. The role of the "trainer" or facilitator is to provide a framework and a context in which professionals can examine their program practices as they relate to a family-centered approach. Through this process of self-examination, professionals continually try to describe what their program is doing right now, how that compares to a family-focused or family-centered approach, and whether a change is needed. Six key questions drive all of the activities:

1. What is our philosophy about working with families?

2. How will we involve families in child assessment?

3. How will we assess family resources, priorities and concerns?

4. How will we involve families in team meetings and decision-making?

5. How will we write family goals and the Individualized Family Service Plan?

6. How will we implement the IFSP and coordinate services?

In the remainder of this monograph, these will be referred to as Key Questions. The activities of the workshop are designed around these Key Questions, with approximately one-half day initially devoted to each. In addition, within each Key Question are embedded a series of Challenge Questions regarding various program practices and procedures. During the workshops, individuals and teams are asked to consider each of the questions.

The ultimate goal of the activities is for professionals to identify for themselves how they are doing and what changes need to be made. Although a time-consuming activity, in the long run it should be effective since those who must implement the change are assuming ownership for decisions about the change process and how it is to occur.

Guided Decision-Making Activities

Making informed decisions about program change requires information about best practices, rules and regulations that will need to be followed, and a structure for guiding group discussion and decision-making activities. In order to facilitate this process, a format has been developed that includes three components: (1) presentation by a facilitator of information and issues related to each of the Key Questions, (2) a case study discussion that highlights some of the issues embedded within each question, and (3) semi-structured small group discussions and decision-making. The workshops are organized such that these activities are provided for each of the six Key Questions.

Presentation and large group discussion led by a facilitator. The primary goal of this activity is to provide participants with enough background information to facilitate good decision-making. Three components are addressed within each presentation. First, the relevant rules and regulations from P. L. 99-457 are presented. If the state in which the workshop is being conducted has made relevant legislative or regulatory decisions, that information is included as well. Second, information about best practices related to the Key Question being discussed (e. g., How will we assess family needs and resources?) are presented so that participants will have at least some information about alternative courses of action and choices that could be made. Finally, the presentation includes a discussion of some of the issues that underlie any decisions that will be made. For example, the discussion might focus on ways in which assessing family needs could be perceived by families as helpful versus intrusive.

The presentation is designed to take 75–90 minutes for each of the six Key Questions, and can be conducted in a large group format with several teams present. Although it is primarily a facilitator-led activity, the topics usually generate a great deal of group discussion and questions. Discussion among participants is important for several reasons. Initially it serves as an "icebreaker"; in addition, the discussion serves to personalize the issues and allows participants the opportunity to share ideas and concerns they may have. More importantly, it sets the stage for future activities by emphasizing the importance of group discussion and participation, and provides a critical opportunity for the facilitator to model strategies for responding to ideas and concerns expressed by participants. As discussed later in the leadership section, the facilitator's role in stimulating and responding to this discussion is essential to the success of this activity.

Case study discussion. The primary goal of this activity is to provide participants an opportunity to apply and discuss issues in the context of a specific family and their interactions with an early intervention program. Although examples of issues and their application inevitably will emerge during the initial facilitator-led presentation, we have written or compiled several case studies designed specifically to challenge professionals to consider how they might implement a family-centered philosophy in working with a particular family (McWilliam & Bailey, in press). Of course, you may want to develop your own case studies as well.

Each case study should be a relatively short (4–10 pages) description of a family and a particular set of issues faced by family members and the professionals working in the program(s) serving the family. The case studies should be based on the actual experiences of early interventionists in the field and represent the types of situations likely to be encountered by most early interventionists at some time in their work with this population. Most importantly, the cases should not provide an answer to the conflicts faced by the professional(s) involved in the cases. Arriving at a solution or course of action for the professionals involved in the case is the objective of the discussion.

Case study discussion provides a common case for all participants to explore and attempt to apply the general principles of a family-centered approach. Although participants may wholeheartedly agree with the principles during the prior presentation and general discussion, attempts to apply the principles to the case study often result in realizations of their own personal biases and values as well as differences in interpretation of the principles among participants (i. e., team members) when it comes down to a specific case situation. Case study discussions are often quite lively and a challenge for the facilitator to keep the discussion on track. General guidelines for facilitating case discussion are provided in this monograph.

The case study discussion usually is conducted with the entire group attending the workshop (assuming that no more than 50 persons are present). Participants need to have read the case study prior to the discussion, however, so its distribution at least one day before the workshop is important. The case study discussion can be as short or as long as the facilitator and the participants prefer. Given time constraints and the amount of material to be covered, we usually limit the case study discussion to one hour.

Small-group discussion and decision-making. The third activity involves teams in small-group discussions and provides a framework for initial decision-making related to each Key Question. The large group is divided into work teams for this activity. It is essential that small group participants include all of those individuals who work together or define themselves as a "team" in the provision of early intervention services. In addition, key administrators, supervisors, or other administrators should be present if at all possible.

For this activity, a set of specific "Challenge Questions" is presented for each of the Key Questions. For example, the Challenge Questions for Key Question #3 (How will we assess family resources, priorities and concerns?) are as follows:

1. Are we complying with all P. L. 99-457 regulations regarding family assessment?

2. Do parents know that we are responsive to family resources, priorities and concerns?

3. Do we try to determine family preferences regarding family assessment?

4. Have we agreed on a flexible model and alternative procedures for assessing family resources, priorities and concerns?

5. Is family assessment recognized as a part of each team member's role?

6. Does each team member have the skills needed to communicate effectively with families?

The Challenge Questions are designed to provide examples of how a family-centered approach might be operationalized and to force team members to examine several dimensions of their program's practices and policies. Prior to the small group discussion, participants are given work sheets on which they indicate whether they think their program needs to change something in response to each of the challenge questions and rank each change in order of perceived importance. The group discussion then involves a sharing of individual rankings, with the goal being group consensus as to areas in which change is needed and a ranking of group priorities. If time is available, the group also operationalizes the type of change needed, sets goals, and identifies resources that are needed in order to facilitate change.

The workshop format that we follow usually does not allow for a full discussion of these issues, since only one hour is allocated for the activity. If Challenge Questions for two Key Questions must be addressed in this one hour period, we have found that this provides only enough time to identify and prioritize needed areas of change. This emphasizes the importance of recognizing this as a beginning activity that will serve as a stimulus and a model for ongoing team discussion and decision-making.

Suggested time frame for activities. The activities described above could be provided in a variety of ways and for varying lengths of time. The schedule reflects an organizational format provided on four separate days that we have found to be workable.

The activities may be lengthened or shortened depending upon the amount of time available. Our experiences have suggested, however, that the time framework described above represents the minimum amount of time needed to begin the planning process. We have also found that trying to do it all in a four-day block is tiring and perhaps not the most effective approach. Breaking it up into two or more segments allows time for further thinking and discussion of the issues and prevents the fatigue that can be a factor after two or three days of intensive work.

Suggested Schedule of Activities

Mornings	*Afternoons*
Day 1	
Facilitator-led discussion: Key Question #1–What is our philosophy about working with families? (90 min.) Facilitator-led discussion: Key Question #2–How will we involve families in child assessment? (90 min.)	Case Study discussion (60 min.) Small group decision-making and goal-setting regarding Key Questions 1 & 2 (75 min.) Large group sharing of major decisions made in small groups (45 min.)
Day 2	
Facilitator-led discussion: Key Question #3–How will we assess family resources, priorities and concerns? (90 min.) Facilitator-led discussion: Key Question #4–How will we involve families in team meetings & decision-making? (90 min.)	Case study discussion (60 min.) Small group decision-making and goal-setting regarding Key Questions 3 & 4 (75 min.) Large group sharing of decisions made in small groups (45 min.)
Day 3	
Facilitator-led discussion: Key Question #5–How will we write family goals and the IFSP? (120 min.) Small group review of sample IFSPs (60 min.)	Large group discussion of small group findings (60 min.) Large group brainstorming about desirable formats (30 min.) Small group discussion of Challenge Questions (60 min.) Large group sharing of decisions made in small groups (30 min.)
Day 4	
Facilitator-led discussion: Key Question #6–How will we implement the IFSP and coordinate services? (90 min.) Case study discussion (45 min.) Small group decision-making and goal-setting regarding Key Question #6 (45 min.)	Small group decision-making and goal-setting, integrating decisions made across the six Key Questions (120 min.) Planning the next steps (60 min.)

Detailed descriptions and guidelines for conducting each component are described in the second section of this monograph.

Goal-Setting

A key aspect of the decision-making process is goal-setting. Ample research in business and education suggests that when organizations set specific goals, change is more likely to occur. Because of the sometimes nebulous nature of a family-centered approach to services, the setting of specific goals becomes even more important. The primary outcome of the small group discussion and decision-making sessions is an identification of needed areas of change and a ranking of priorities within each Key Question. The purpose of the last afternoon's session is twofold: (1) to look across the seven Key Questions and identify top priority areas for focusing the change process, and (2) to set specific goals for change and identify resources and strategies needed in order to achieve them.

Even by devoting an entire afternoon to this process, however, a detailed plan will not be completed. The workshop will merely provide a beginning for what will likely be an extended endeavor in which goals are identified, resources negotiated, and strategies tried until desired levels of change are achieved.

Core Reading Assignments

Extensive reading assignments prior to the workshop generally are not appropriate, since participants usually have busy schedules and many competing demands for their time. A small set of core readings, however, can (a) establish a common base of information prior to the workshop, (b) stimulate thinking about issues relevant to the workshop content, and (c) provide concrete examples of principles, instruments, forms, and procedures that can serve as a basis for discussions and as a resource for future reference.

Selection of readings is the prerogative of the facilitator and should be based on current readings relevant to the groups participating in the workshops. We have found one reference, *Guidelines and Recommended Practices for the Individualized Family Service Plan* (Johnson, McGonigel, & Kaufmann, 1989; 1991), to be especially useful, for several reasons: (a) it was developed by a national task force comprised of parents and professionals from a variety of agencies and programs, and represents a consensus of opinion about best practice; (b) it is relatively short and very readable; and (c) it contains several case studies, examples of IFSP formats, sample assessment tools, and practical guidelines for translating principles into practices.

Suggested readings from this reference are included with each module description in Section II. Since two editions of the document exist, we have provided references for both. Also, a list of other recommended readings for participants and leaders is included.

Effective Leadership

The qualities and skills of the facilitator are an important aspect of the activities described in this manual. We have provided a broad structure and a series of activities for the workshop. There is considerable flexibility, however, in how the content is presented, and each workshop and each group of participants will be different. The following attributes seem to be important in effective leadership:

1. The facilitator must have some background and experiences in working with young children with disabilities and their families. By sharing experiences and giving examples, the facilitator can bring to life many of the issues being discussed. Those experiences and examples must, however, relate to the experiences of the participants.

2. The facilitator must be familiar with Public Law 99-457, the regulations accompanying the law, and current or proposed rules and regulations for the state in which the workshop is being held. In addition, the facilitator needs to be familiar with major issues, trends, and procedures that have been discussed in the professional literature. Although the workshop is not designed to teach skills, the effectiveness of the leader in facilitating the discussion and decision-making process will depend in part upon the participants' perception of the facilitator as a person who is knowledgeable about best practices and issues surrounding implementation of a family focus.

3. The facilitator must be able to engage participants actively in the workshop through use of effective questioning skills or by posing credible dilemmas to which the participants are expected to respond.

4. The facilitator must be flexible and able to think on his or her feet. The activities will inevitably generate considerable discussion. Participants will give examples of families with whom they have worked that have posed challenges for them and will question the meaning of a family-centered approach with them. The facilitator must be able to accept all concerns as legitimate and be able to help participants see for themselves the relevance of a family-centered approach. This necessitates a nonjudgmental attitude, the ability to respond empathetically, and skills in engaging other participants in problem solving.

5. The facilitator must be able to set aside his or her own priorities for the participating teams and allow them to establish priorities for change as they see fit. This may be difficult in some cases, especially if the facilitator has strong ideas about what should be done, but the facilitator must realize that change is unlikely if priorities are imposed from the outside. Allowing teams to establish their own goals and priorities helps give teams ownership of the change process. If they succeed in areas they have identified, they may then move into other areas.

6. Ultimately it is important for the facilitator to model for participants the same attitude and skills that participants should have in working with families.

Chapter III
Preparing for the Workshop

W<small>ORKSHOP SUCCESS</small> will depend heavily on preworkshop planning and preparation. This section describes some of the factors that should be taken into consideration.

Deciding Who Will Attend

An initial consideration is identifying the target audience. Obviously this will vary according to the purpose of the workshop and the agency that sponsors it. Of importance, however, is to begin by asking what teams, programs, or geographical areas are to be included. The workshop and activities planned rest on the assumption that the participants work together in some way and must make common decisions about program practices and program changes. The target groups could be as specific as staff from several home-based infant intervention teams in adjacent counties, several center-based programs, or several hospital units. Or, it could be as broad as all of the agencies providing infant and toddler services within a particular town, county, or other geographical region. There should be some type of common denominator across the groups; otherwise, the effectiveness of the discussion, decision-making, and sharing activities will be diminished.

Once target groups have been identified, the next step is to identify all of the individual participants who will attend. Some programs take the approach of sending one or two designated staff to a workshop, with the expectation that they will convey key concepts to other program staff. That model will not work in the case of this workshop. It is essential that all team members participate in the full range of activities. The workshops inevitably will challenge current program and individual practices. The discussion that occurs and the decisions that are made will likely have a significant impact on the way services are provided and the way professionals approach their work with families. If this experience is provided for only a portion of the staff, change will be less likely; if change does occur, it may be without the input or assent of some staff, resulting in discrepancies in services or philosophy within a program or agency.

Participants should include full-time, part-time, and consulting staff. Part-time and consulting staff, such as physical or occupational therapists, nurses, social workers, physicians, psychologists, and speech-language pathologists, often are not included in training; yet the ways they interact with families reflect upon the program as a whole and are an essential part of the messages that families receive from programs.

No more than 50–60 persons should attend the workshop, and 20–25 are preferable. Large group discussion is compromised when too many people are present, and this discussion is important to the effectiveness of the experience.

Identifying Facilitators

The facilitator(s) are another important key to workshop success. As described in Chapter II, the facilitator should (a) have clinical experiences in working with young children with disabilities and their families, (b) be familiar with the law, the regulations, and major issues, trends, and practices in working with families, (c) be able to engage participants in effective discussions, (d) be able to think fast and respond appropriately to an array of questions, concerns, and comments, and (e) be willing to allow teams to set their own priorities for change. The facilitator should also be familiar with the laws and regulations within the state and region served by the participants, the types of service models represented (e. g., home-based, NICU, day care), and special regional considerations regarding cultural diversity.

The number of facilitators may vary. The workshop could be conducted by one person. There are several advantages, however, to having two facilitators. It creates diversity for the participants and a break for the facilitator. Furthermore, two facilitators can bring different strengths and experiences to the workshop and can support each other in preparing for and evaluating workshop activities.

One model would be to have one facilitator be an individual who is external to the region or agency (e. g., a state department representative, university faculty person, technical assistance coordinator, consultant, or service provider from another region) and the other to be a local agency representative. This provides a balance of having a "neutral" outsider and an "invested" insider. Both persons should be individuals who would be respected by participants as knowledgeable and effective leaders. If the local region is characterized by two strongly different "camps" with respect to program philosophy or services, it is essential that the local person not be aligned with either camp. In this case, it may be best to have both facilitators be outsiders. Another model would be to have a parent as one of the facilitators or co-facilitators. Although we have not tried this model ourselves, it is likely to be effective if well-planned.

Although any number of models could be used for the facilitators, it is important that one or more local persons have responsibility for providing leadership and assistance in planning the workshop and in facilitating the continuation of planning and decision-making after the workshop is over.

Preparation For Facilitators
Facilitators will need to do several things in preparation for the workshop. Among these are:

1. Read this manual and become familiar with its content.

2. Read the recommended references associated with each module.

3. Prepare activities for each workshop component.

4. Practice before implementing.

5. Collaborate with co-facilitators in order to ensure continuity.

This manual is designed to provide a framework and structure for the workshop. It is not our expectation, however, that the guidelines provided here would be followed rigidly in every site. Facilitators should view this as a resource for designing an individualized workshop experience that meets the needs of local teams and fits their presentation style and preferences.

Contacting Participants

Communication with participants prior to the workshop is important. All persons attending the workshop must have a clear understanding of the goals and format of the workshop, expectations of participants, and anticipated outcomes. They should know who will attend and it should be clear that the workshop is an important beginning of a long-term process of self-examination, goal-setting, and change. Pre-workshop communication should also let participants know that the activity is endorsed by key decision-makers and that their efforts will, in fact, make a difference.

Pre-workshop communication can take many forms, including announcements at staff meetings, letters from facilitators and key program personnel, and special meetings called to discuss plans and procedures. A combination of these activities will ensure that all participants begin the workshop with a shared understanding of its purpose and format.

Deciding on a Schedule

How much time will be devoted to the workshop and how will that time be distributed? The answer to this question will vary widely across programs and communities, and will depend upon resources available, time constraints of the facilitators, and demands for service delivery. Our experiences suggest that four days are needed to cover the range of topics and to provide sufficient time for discussion and initial planning activities. [In one state we used a two-day format, and many participants said that the time allocated was insufficient.] On the other hand, four consecutive days is intense and may not be possible for many programs. We recommend that each component of the workshop be at least one day in length, divided into two two-day workshops or four one-day workshops. The total time from the first to the last workshop, however, probably should not exceed two or three months.

Within each workshop day, approximately six hours of activities are suggested. The distribution of this time, of course, may vary according to local needs and schedules.

Preparing for Family Participation

One important decision is whether to invite families to participate in the training. Our research and experiences suggest that parents can contribute significantly to the workshop and that both parents and professionals view parent participation as a positive experience. The decision to invite parents should be jointly determined by facilitators and staff, so that everyone agrees on it. The number of parents to invite is certainly a local option. We believe that each team or program should have parent representation, and that more than one parent should attend. In previous workshops we have conducted, we have invited two parents for every six professionals, a ratio that seemed to work well.

Assuming that the decision has been made to invite family members to participate, several activities need to occur. First, families will need to be identified as candidates for participation. This decision must be individualized according to programs and families served. We have found that it works best if the parents attending are those who are currently receiving services from the program, but who have been a part of the program for at least a year. Also, since the number of parents present is small relative to the total number served, it is important to invite family members who could serve as representatives of the broad array of families served by the program.

It is extremely difficult for parents to commit four days to this workshop. Many work and all have busy schedules. Also, finding satisfactory child care is almost always an issue. Our efforts at involving parents have been most successful when we have provided assistance with child care and have compensated families for their time.

Families and professionals need to be aware of why they have been invited and what their role is to be. It is important that families be given equal status with professionals for this activity. They should be able to speak whenever they wish and to contribute to the discussion and decision-making in the same way as do professionals. This needs to be communicated prior to the workshop.

During the workshop, it is helpful if the facilitator sets aside a brief time to meet with parents to assess how they perceive the events that have transpired thus far. At the end of the first day is a good time for this. The meeting need not be a long one, but sometimes parents are disturbed by some of the things they hear professionals saying. Also, the workshop often results in parents' examining their own roles with the agency and with their child. Giving them an opportunity to discuss any concerns with the facilitator can help provide support and perhaps can influence planning for subsequent workshop activities.

Space and Furnishings

Certain features of the physical environment will influence the extent to which the workshop is both enjoyable and effective. Factors such as temperature, lighting, external noise, other distractions, and ability to hear the presenter must be considered and addressed. If possible, the workshop should be conducted away from the office in order to provide a "retreat" atmosphere and to avoid the temptation to answer the phone or see visitors. Ideally, participants should sit at one or more tables, rather than just in rows of chairs. This gives a more professional feel to the workshop and helps in note-taking and reference to written materials. The building should have a sufficient number of rooms or private areas so that each team or small group has a place to meet and discuss issues in a distraction-free environment.

Advance Readings and Preparation of Materials

The workshop is enhanced if participants do some reading in advance. This means that whatever reading material is expected should be distributed well ahead of time. Also, a written schedule of expected readings should be distributed to all participants. During the workshop, remind participants of what readings are expected for the next session.

As facilitators read through the modules, it will become apparent that several materials will need to be prepared. This manual provides figures that can be used as overhead transparencies. These will need to be prepared and organized prior to the training, and arrangements made for an overhead projector, screen, and extension cord. Also, we have included forms for facilitating small group decision-making, outlines for each module, and other handouts that may be helpful for participants. Facilitators will need to decide what handouts are desirable and insure that sufficient copies have been made of each prior to the workshop.

Preparation for Case Study Discussion

The major task of the facilitator in preparing for case study discussion is the selection of an appropriate case. Case selection is dependent on a number of factors including the purpose for using the case (i. e., instructional objectives, topic covered), the amount of time available for case discussion, the skill level of workshop participants, the amount of time participants have to prepare for case discussion, and the comparability of the case to the types of children and families the participants have encountered or are likely to encounter in their own work place.

If you are intimately involved with the program in which the participants work (e. g., you are a director or supervisor), you may elect to use a situation involving a child and family from the program's actual caseload. If all the participants are equally aware of the details of the case, this may be a good decision, in that the participants will see the immediate applicability of the principles to their own work. Even so, there may be disadvantages to selecting such a case. First, issues of confidentiality must be considered, especially if you have decided to have families or representatives from other agencies participate in the workshop. Second, some decisions about the case have probably already been made by team members. This may result in embarrassment or defensiveness on the part of these participants in the course of discussion.

Often it is desirable to select a case that is new to all participants. The cases we have written and used in our own training or solicited from other authors are available in *Children, families, and communities of caring: Case studies in early intervention* McWilliam and Bailey (in press). You may also use cases from other sources or decide to write your own. Whatever case you use, the most important criteria is that the case does not state or imply a solution to the situation described. The purpose of case method discussion is to guide trainees through the **process** of arriving at a course of action they would take if they were the professional(s) in the case.

Depending upon your schedule of training, you may choose to use a different case for each module or use one case to cover two or more content areas. Just be certain that the case is appropriate for the content area(s) covered.

Other tasks involved in preparing for case study discussion are as follows:

• *Know the Case in Detail*

Read the case well in advance of the workshop and remember it in detail. It is best not to have to rely on notes or the case itself during the discussion. Your attention must be on what the participants are saying.

• *Prepare Participants for Case Discussion*

Ensure that participants are aware of the purpose of the case study discussion and be certain that they have adequate time to read and think about the case prior to the discussion.

• *Prepare Discussion Questions*

Write a list of questions you might pose to participants to guide them through the process of applying the principles you are concerned with to the case at hand. Keep in mind that open-ended questions generate more discussion than closed-ended questions. Use these questions to start the discussion, to rejuvenate a faltering discussion, or to redirect the discussion back to the case at hand if it gets off track.

• *Read Guidelines for Facilitating Case Discussions*

A list of general guidelines and strategies for leading group discussion of cases is provided in Appendix A of this monograph. These guidelines have been culled from the literature on case method instruction as well as from our own experiences in incorporating case study discussion in the training of early intervention professionals.

Planning for Small-Group Decision-Making and Goal-Setting

The purpose of the presentations and case study discussions is to provide participants the beginnings of a common background for program planning and decision making. At the end of Days 1, 2, and 3, and the morning of Day 4, participants are asked to begin identifying needs for change and establish some priorities. The afternoon of Day 4 is devoted to synthesizing these decisions and developing a team plan for system change.

The small-group activities center around sets of Challenge Questions designed to go along with each Key Question. The way that we have worked this process is as follows:

1. After the case study discussion, distribute copies of the key questions related to the day's topics to each participant. [Copies of these forms are included in the next section of this manual.] For example, after the case study discussion on Day 1, distribute the Challenge Questions for Key Question 1 (What is our philosophy of working with families?) and Key Question 2 (How will we involve families in child assessment?).

2. Have participants respond to each challenge question by indicating whether they feel there is a need for change and assigning a priority ranking to each change. If time allows, there is also a space on the forms for participants to make notes about the specific type of change needed or to identify potential resources for making the change a reality.

3. Once individuals have completed their forms, divide the group into teams. For approximately one hour, the teams should meet to agree on needed changes and develop a shared priority ranking for each Key Question. It is unlikely that a plan for change can be made in this short period of time, but usually it is sufficient to identify the major changes and prioritize them. The teams will need to be encouraged to work efficiently during this time.

4. We generally let teams decide for themselves how to organize and structure the hour, so long as they focus on the task. Encourage them to identify a note taker and a facilitator. In some teams, the team leader will be the facilitator, whereas in others the responsibility may rotate.

5. After the small group discussions, get the teams back into a large group. Have each team share with the others the major topics of discussion and decisions that were made.

Although the small group activities could possibly be conducted without a formal structure, we have found that the provision of a specific form helps facilitate the process. A set of suggested forms is provided in Section II. It may be important to modify these in accordance with local needs or issues.

Evaluating Workshop Activities

Most workshops are evaluated using measures of participant satisfaction. Of importance, however, is the extent to which the workshop achieved its goals. Because each workshop may have a different set of expectations or goals, it is often important to design an individualized evaluation plan. We suggest that at least three types of evaluation data be gathered: Follow-up assessments of practices, goal attainment, and participant satisfaction.

Follow-up assessments of practices. One way to evaluate the workshop is to use some standard measure of the family-centered practices in a given program or community. We have developed the FOCAS (Family Orientation of Community and Agency Services) instrument as one mechanism for conducting such an assessment. A copy of the measure is included in Appendix B. The purpose of the FOCAS scale is to determine individual perceptions of how families are included in a given early intervention program. The scale consists of 12 items addressing various program components, with two items for each of the six Key Questions. We have used the FOCAS in two ways. First, by documenting discrepancies between current and desired practices, we have helped establish the need for this workshop. We have gathered FOCAS data in seven states, and in each case have found a substantial discrepancy between typical and desired practices. Second, the FOCAS instrument has been used as a follow-up assessment to determine broad-based program changes. One phenomenon we have found is that if the FOCAS is administered immediately after the workshop, ratings of current practices decline. This probably means that the workshop helped participants examine current practices in a critical fashion and served to identify areas of practice in which professionals were not as family-centered as they thought. In a six-month follow-up, however, we found that teams who had participated in the training reported significant changes in practices in a direction of becoming more family-centered.

Goal attainment. A direct measure of workshop effectiveness is documentation of the extent to which goals established in the workshop were attained.

This requires that participants write down identified goals and at some point in time examine goal attainment. A six-month interval is a reasonable period of time in which to do some initial examination of goal attainment. The goals that will be listed using Handout 7-1 can form the basis for determining the extent to which goals have been achieved.

Participant satisfaction. Although the ultimate test of any workshop is the extent to which change occurs, documenting participant satisfaction is helpful for planning future training activities. Some suggested forms for assessing satisfaction are included in Appendix C.

SECTION II:
Guidelines
& Materials for
Conducting the Workshop

What is Our Philosophy About Working with Families?

THE FIRST SESSION is designed to provide an orientation to the purpose and format of the workshop and help participants realize that becoming family-centered is a decision that needs to be made within the context of a total program philosophy. The specific goals are for participants to:

1. Understand the purpose of the workshop and the activities planned to achieve that purpose.

2. Know the basic philosophical premises underlying a family-centered approach to early intervention.

3. Know the aspects of P. L. 99-457 that provide guidance in developing a philosophy of services based on a family-centered approach.

4. Identify key issues associated with developing and implementing a family-centered philosophy.

Suggested Readings for the Facilitator

Bailey, D. B. (1987). Collaborative goal setting with families: Resolving differences in values and priorities for services. *Topics in Early Childhood Special Education, 7*(2), 59-71.

Bernheimer, L. P., Gallimore, R., & Weisner, T. S. (1990). Ecocultural theory as a context for the Individual Family Service Plan. *Journal of Early Intervention, 14,* 219-233.

Brewer, E. J., McPherson, M., Magrab, P. R., & Hutchins, V. L. (1989). Family-centered, community-based, coordinated care for children with special health care needs. *Pediatrics, 83,* 1055-1060.

Dunst, C. J., Trivette, C., & Deal, A. (1988). *Enabling and empowering families: Principles and guidelines for practice.* Cambridge, MA: Brookline Books.

Espe-Sherwindt, M., & Kerlin, S. L. (1990). Early intervention with parents with mental retardation: Do we empower or impair? *Infants and Young Children, 2*(4), 21-28.

Suggested Readings for Participants

Johnson, B. H., McGonigel, M. J., & Kaufmann, R. K. (1989; 1991). *Guidelines and recommended practices for the individualized family service plan.* Bethesda, MD: American Association for the Care of Children's Health.

1989 Edition	*1991 Edition*
1. Chapters 1-3 (pp. 1-21)	1. Chapters 1-3 (pp. 1-28)
2. Appendix B	2. Appendix B
3. Appendix C	

Suggested Outline of Session

Since this is the first session, some introductions will probably be needed, especially if the facilitator is not a part of the program, or if multiple program sites are represented.

HANDOUT 1-1 follows this section as a possible outline for the facilitator and the participants. Throughout this section are the major headings of the outline, followed by some suggestions for points to be made or questions to stimulate discussion. Reference is made to overheads or other handouts that might be useful and copies of these are also included at the end of this section.

 I. Why have a workshop on becoming family-centered?

Although participants should already have information about the workshop, some background information and a reminder of the expectations for the workshop are important.

I.A. P. L. 99-457: Legislative foundations for a family-centered approach in early intervention

Researchers, practitioners, and family members have been writing about being more responsive to families for several years. Many early intervention personnel would argue that their work has always been family-centered. P. L. 99-457 and P. L. 102-119, however, have forced programs to rethink their basic mission. The requirements for the IFSP are the most visible ways in which the law mandates a family-centered approach. TRANSPARENCY 1-1 lists the major requirements for the IFSP.

 I.B. Changing ideas about what it means to be family-centered

Research over the past decade suggests that some practices that we thought were family-centered may not have been viewed as supportive by all families. *DISCUSSION QUESTION: Can you think of examples of practices that were intended to be supportive of families but turned out not to be?* Common examples may include parent group meetings that nobody attends or home-based teaching or therapeutic activities that parents don't implement. *DISCUSSION QUESTION: Why do you think parents did not participate in these activities?* Although many factors influence family choices, a likely explanation is that the activities did not meet individual family needs or were not consistent with family priorities. Current views of family-centered care emphasize program practices that vary according to parent preferences and reinforce family choices.

 I.C. The IFSP is but one indication of a family-centered approach; ideally it should permeate all facets of early intervention.

The point to be made here is that the use of an IFSP form does not ensure that a program is family-centered. Every encounter that a family has with an agency, program, or professional sends messages about the extent to which family values, capabilities, and resources are valued.

I.D. Research and experience suggest that changing early intervention services to include a focus on families is a challenging and difficult task.

Several studies, as well as reports from parents and professionals have suggested that there is a discrepancy between current and desired practices in working with families. Also, efforts to change programs to a family-centered approach have often met with numerous barriers to change. *DISCUSSION QUESTION: What do you think are some of the factors that make change to family-centered services difficult?* Among the major factors likely to be mentioned are (1) college and university programs that focus primarily on work with children, (2) lack of well-defined models and definitions of a "family-centered approach", (3) administrative barriers, (4) perceived and real family barriers, (5) personal philosophies about work and appropriate professional roles.

 I. E. How can this change be accomplished?

Given the magnitude of change expected and the many barriers that exist, a realistic question is how can this all happen? Research on the change process suggests the following:

1. Change is always difficult
2. Change is an ongoing activity and should be expected
3. Support throughout the change process is essential
4. Individuals are more likely to respond to initiatives for change if they are provided significant opportunities to make decisions about the nature and direction of change.
5. Setting specific goals for change helps focus the change effort and provides guidelines for evaluating the extent to which the goals for change have been achieved.
6. Involving consumers (in this case, parents) in making decisions about change is likely to result in program policies and procedures that are consistent with expectations for services.

This workshop is designed to help programs set a course for change by identifying areas in which change is needed and developing goals and a plan for their accomplishment.

II. What are some key questions or areas of decision-making for teams?

The first feature of the workshop is a focus on selected dimensions of program practice. The six key questions to be addressed are displayed in TRANSPARENCY 1-2. After a brief discussion of each, ask participants to identify other areas of program practice (e. g., transitions, intake, etc.) where practices ought to be examined.

 III. How will the workshop be organized?

This section provides a brief overview of the workshop activities and reinforces the expectation that it will involve significant discussion and group decision-making. A summary of the major points to be made is provided on TRANSPARENCY 1-3. Emphasize the fact that to a large extent, the group is in charge of its own destiny. Reinforce and re-mind the group of whatever administrative endorsements have been in support of their efforts.

 IV. What is our philosophy about working with families?

This section begins the facilitator-led discussion of the first Key Question, which regards the extent to which a family-centered approach is embedded within the program's philosophy.

 IV.A. Why have a program philosophy?

DISCUSSION QUESTION: Why have a program philosophy? Participants will probably be able to identify the major reasons for having a program philosophy. Be sure that the following points get made:

1. A program philosophy helps guide decisions by establishing standards or aspirations.
2. A philosophy provides a mechanism for ensuring that all staff strive to achieve the same end.
3. A philosophy provides a public statement of a program's approach to early intervention and is essential if consumers are deciding whether or not to make use of a program's services.

IV.B. What is a family-centered philosophy?

Many people have written about a family-focused or family-centered approach to early intervention, but a number of different perspectives have been offered. *DISCUSSION QUESTION: What do you think are the essential aspects of a family-centered philosophy?*

 IV.C. Some examples of philosophy statements or principles

HANDOUT 1-2 provides several definitions, principles, or philosophy statements that have appeared in the literature. Ask participants to read them and then rethink their responses to the discussion question above regarding the essential aspects of a family-centered philosophy.

 IV.D. A summary of some assumptions

By this time the discussion will probably have identified many of the key assumptions underlying a family-centered approach. Our interpretation of this literature is that at least seven assumptions underlie this philosophy. They are listed on the participants' handouts and are displayed on TRANSPARENCY 1-4:

1. *Family-centered:* We recognize that the family is the constant in the child's life while the service systems and personnel within those systems may be involved only episodically.

2. *Ecologically-based:* In our work with families we need to consider the interrelatedness of the various contexts which surround the child and family.

3. *Individualized:* Since the needs of each child and each family differ, services should be individualized to meet those unique needs.

4. *Culturally sensitive:* Families come from different cultures and ethnic groups. families reflect their diversity in their views and

expectations of themselves, of their children and of professionals. Services should be provided in ways that are sensitive to these variations and consistent with family values and beliefs.

5. *Enabling and empowering:* Services should foster a family's independence, existing and developing skills, and sense of competence and worth.

6. *Needs-based:* A "needs-based" approach starts with a family's expressed interests and collaborates with families in identifying and obtaining services according to their priorities.

7. *Coordinated service delivery:* Families need access to a well-coordinated system of services.

8. *Normalized:* Programs work to promote the integration of the child and the family within the community

9. *Collaborative:* Early intervention services should be based on a collaborative relationship between families and professionals.

 ## IV.E. Some issues in developing a program philosophy

Several issues need to be considered in the context of developing a program philosophy. The purpose of this section is to provide opportunities for discussing those issues as they pertain to the participants.

 ## IV.E.1. Philosophy vs. policies vs. regulations

DISCUSSION QUESTION: What differentiates a philosophy statement from policies and procedures? In general, a philosophy statement should be relatively brief and should convey beliefs, concepts, or attitudes regarding the delivery of services. Policies and regulations provide operational guidelines for implementing those beliefs.

IV.E.2. Individual beliefs vs. program philosophy

DISCUSSION QUESTION: Does each staff member have to "believe in" the program philosophy? Obviously each professional has a set of fundamental beliefs about who they are and what the proper relationship is between professionals and families. A philosophy statement should allow for some diversity, but also should set some standards or parameters for professional practice. It is likely that this discussion will turn to the question of whether it is appropriate for someone who does not believe in a family-centered approach to work in early intervention.

 IV.E.3. Who establishes the program philosophy in your program?

DISCUSSION QUESTION: Do you as a group have the authority to make or change the program's philosophy? We have witnessed the unfortunate situation in which workshop participants decided they wanted to develop a revised philosophy statement and did so, only to be told that the executive board was the only legitimate group to establish or change the philosophy statement. This points to the importance of involving administrators in planning the workshop and allowing participants an avenue for shaping change. This part of the workshop might turn to a discussion of the proper channels or strategies for changing program philosophy.

 IV.E.4. Applying the philosophy in daily interactions between staff and families

DISCUSSION QUESTION: Does a philosophy statement make any real difference in what people do? The discussion might begin by asking whether the current philosophy (if there is one) has any effect on professional practices. The discussion should then turn to a consideration of factors necessary to ensure that all staff implement the philosophy and that program practices actually reflect that philosophy.

 IV.E.5. Communicating a program's philosophy

DISCUSSION QUESTION: Are families and other agencies currently aware of our philosophy (if there is one)? If pressed, could all staff articulate the key elements of the program philosophy? The discussion here should focus on strategies for publicizing the philosophy and for frequently reminding staff of key philosophical assumptions.

 ## IV. F. Some challenge questions

Handout 1-3 presents seven Challenge Questions about program philosophy. These should be introduced to participants as the questions that initially will drive their decision-making about program change. Orient them to the form and briefly discuss each question.

Key Question 2:
How Will We Involve Families in Child Assessment?

THE CHILD ASSESSMENT PROCESS represents one of the first opportunities for examining existing practices to determine the need for a more family-centered approach. This component of the workshop provides teams with information needed to develop a plan for offering families opportunities to be involved in the assessment of their children. The specific goals are for participants to:

1. Know P. L. 99-457 rules and regulations related to the assessment of infants and toddlers.

2. Develop a rationale for involving family members as partners in child assessment.

3. Recognize that families will vary in the ways and extent to which they wish to be involved in child assessment, and identify a range of options for finding out how families want to be involved.

4. Describe a variety of ways in which families could be involved in planning and conducting child assessments.

5. Recognize that families may have different goals and priorities for their children than do professionals, and discuss strategies to resolve those differences in a mutually satisfactory fashion.

6. Discuss the importance of documenting child strengths and describe strategies for identifying and building on strengths.

Suggested Readings for the Facilitator

Bailey, D. B., & Wolery, M. (1989). Assessment and its importance in early intervention. In *Assessing infants and preschoolers with handicaps* (pp. 1-21). Columbus, OH: Merrill Publishing Co.

Brinkerhoff, J. L., & Vincent, L. J. (1986). Increasing parental decision making at the individualized educational program meeting. *Journal of the Division for Early Childhood, 11,* 46-58.

Kjerland, L., & Kovach, J. (1990). Family-staff collaboration for tailored infant assessment. In E. D. Gibbs & D. M. Teti (Eds.) , *Interdisciplinary assessment of infants (*pp. 287-298). Baltimore, MD: Paul H. Brookes Publishing Co.

Squires, J. K., Nickel, R., & Bricker, D. (1990). Use of parent-completed developmental questionnaires for child-find and screening. *Infants and Young Children, 3*(2), 46-57.

Suggested Readings for Participants

Johnson, B. H., McGonigel, M. J., & Kaufmann, R. K. (1989; 1991). *Guidelines and recommended practices for the individualized family service plan.* Bethesda, MD: Association for the Care of Children's Health.

1989 Edition	*1991 Edition*
1. Chapter 5, pp. 31-36	1. Chapter 5
2. Appendix D	2. Appendix C

Suggested Outline of Session

A suggested outline for participants to follow is presented in HANDOUT 2-1. This section follows that outline and presents suggestions for points to be made under each major heading.

 I. P. L. 99-457 regulations related to child assessment

The major provisions of P. L. 99-457 related to child assessment are displayed in TRANSPARENCY 2-1. Each point should be summarized, indicating both the specificity and generality of the provisions. For example, the law states that the evaluation must be comprehensive and multidisciplinary, yet multidisciplinary is defined as two or more professions. Several important points are:

1. The difference between evaluation (for determining eligibility) and assessment (for determining service needs).

2. The five key areas required in all assessments. Note that the labels for these areas have been changed as a result of P. L. 102-119. (Language/speech = Communication, Psychological = Social/Emotional and Self-help = Adaptive)

3. Assessment of each child's unique needs.

4. An explicit recognition of the importance of "informed clinical judgment." Related to this, the comments following the regulations in the *Federal Register* state that "since standardized diagnostic instruments are generally unavailable for use with infants and toddlers with handicaps, the Secretary believes that the evaluation of children under this part must be based on informed clinical opinion." (June 26, 1989, p. 26333)

5. Assessment of strengths must now be included

6. P. L. 102-119 states that infant assessments must be family-directed.

7. The 45-day timeline is calendar days, not working days.

The amendments do not clarify what is meant by "family-directed" assessments. However, because child assessment is one of the first ways in which programs interact with families, programs should examine the extent to which child assessment practices are family centered.

II. Rationale for family involvement in child assessment.

One way to begin this discussion is by showing the quote by Bronfenbrenner displayed in TRANSPARENCY 2-2. Although this quote is in reference to developmental psychology, in some ways it characterizes a traditional approach to child assessment in schools, diagnostic clinics, and early intervention programs.

 II.A. Characteristics of traditional assessment processes.

DISCUSSION QUESTION: What are some characteristics of a traditional approach to the assessment of young children with disabilities? TRANSPARENCY 2-3 lists some of the major characteristics that might be mentioned and provides space for writing in others. As each is mentioned, ask for or give clinical examples. An important point to make at the end of this section is that these practices evolved for a number of important reasons: (1) professionals have a lot of specialized knowledge and training, (2) tests provide important normative information, (3) there are some advantages of assessment in a controlled or standardized context, (4) standard identification procedures are needed to determine eligibility and placement, and (5) knowledge of deficits or needs is likely to be important in planning intervention goals and activities.

 II.B. Problems/limitations with traditional assessment practices.

Although traditional assessment practices achieve some goals of assessment, other purposes might be thwarted. *DISCUSSION QUESTION: What do you think are some of the limitations of a traditional approach to child assessment?* Some examples of common concerns are displayed in TRANSPARENCY 2-4. Space is provided for writing down other concerns that might be mentioned.

 II.C. Goals of child assessment

Given the limitations described, professionals need to reexamine the purpose of child assessment. *DISCUSSION QUESTION: What do you think are the goals of the child assessment process?*

TRANSPARENCY 2-5 describes an alternative set of goals that add a family-centered component to the child assessment process.

 ## III. Strategies for involving parents in child assessment

If a program wanted to be more family-centered in its child assessment activities, what would it do? This section addresses some possible ways of involving families in this process.

 ## III.A. Determining family goals for the assessment process

Families enter the assessment process wanting different things: a diagnosis, prognosis for the future, eligibility for services, confirmation of concerns, goals for treatment, need for therapy, reasons for behavior, or some estimate of developmental status. One way of being family focused is to determine each family's goals for the assessment process. *DISCUSSION QUESTION: Why would it be important to determine parent goals for child assessment, and how could you go about doing that?*

 ## III.B. Determining family preferences for involvement

Families vary in the extent and ways in which they would like to be involved in child assessment activities. Some prefer to watch, while others would like a more active role. Thus a second strategy for adding a family focus to the child assessment process is to determine family preferences for involvement. Table 1 in the IFSP monograph (Johnson, McGonigel, & Kaufmann, 1989), reproduced in TRANSPARENCY 2-6, gives some ideas of questions that may be asked of caregivers in making this determination.

Facilitators may also want to refer to Appendix D in the IFSP monograph for examples of other ways to involve families in preassessment planning.

What are some roles that families might play in the child assessment process? TRANSPARENCY 2-7 lists some possible roles. A summary of each follows:

1. *Receiver* of information gathered by professionals. This is the traditional role for families, and some may choose only this role. Parents can, of course, play an important role by identifying the kinds of information they would like to receive. Of importance is how that information is conveyed. TRANSPARENCY 2-8 summarizes the findings of study by Cadman, Shurvill, Davies, and Bradfield (1984). These authors found several key factors that influenced the extent to which recommendations generated by an interdisciplinary team were followed by parents and other professionals. At this point, facilitators may also want to refer to the box on page 36 of the monograph entitled "Tips for Discussing Assessment Information with Families." *DISCUSSION QUESTION: If parents play only the receiver role, what are professionals likely to miss in the assessment process?*

2. *Observer* of professional assessments. Having parents present as non-participating observers has at least three advantages. First, by observing what professionals do and how children react, they gain an understanding of how professionals approach the assessment task. Second, the observation gives parents an experiential basis for determining the extent to which their child's behavior in testing reflects behavior in other contexts. Third, the presence of a familiar adult is likely to help the child adapt more easily to the assessment situation and thus the results may more nearly reflect the child's ability.

3. *Informant* about specific behaviors and developmental milestones. A third role for parents is to provide information about specific skills, usually from a checklist developed by professionals. Sometimes entire measures (e. g., Developmental Profile) are

based on parent interview, whereas others (e. g., Battelle Developmental Inventory) use direct testing for some items and parent interview for others. This approach provides useful infor-mation, not only about the child's skills, but the caregiver's perception of those skills. A number of studies have compared parent and professional ratings of children's abilities. Sheehan's (1988) review of the literature concluded that 75% of the studies reported that parents rated children higher than did professionals. *DISCUSSION QUESTION: What do you think this finding means?* The issue is probably not who is right, but what are the unique perspectives that parents and professionals bring to the assessment process. Rather than serving as a point of disagreement, differing perspectives on ability can provide a useful opportunity for discussing how behavior and abilities vary and the factors that influence that variation.

4. *Describer* of parent-generated skills and competencies. Although the informant role is an important one, it only gives parents the opportunity to rate skills or behaviors identified by professionals. In the describer role, parents are asked open-ended question about their children, allowing for a broader range of responses. For example, a closed-ended question such as "Does your child eat with a spoon?" will usually result in a yes-no answer, whereas "What are mealtimes like for you and your child?" opens the door for information not only about skills, but also about the enjoyment or frustration of meals, family routines and expectations, and involvement of significant others.

5. *Interpreter* of child's strengths and needs in the context of family routines and values. In addition to describing children's skills and competencies, family members can also provide information regarding the extent to which they perceive certain skills or deficits to be important. For example, a mother might describe her child's poor feeding skills but indicate that when viewed in context, those needs are not as important as others.

6. *Participant* in gathering data. Some family members may want to participate in various data collection activities themselves. *DISCUSSION QUESTION: What are some examples of ways that family members can participate in data collection? What do you think are the advantages and disadvantages of this?* Some of the ways include naturalistic observation (e. g., observing arrival and departure times), record-keeping (e. g., sleep-wake cycles, nutritional intake), or conducting certain assessments. The arena assessment model (Wolery & Dyk, 1984) provides another opportunity for family members to participate in child assessment:

> *A temporary facilitator, generally the team member with the most expertise in the child's area of need, is assigned prior to the actual assessment activities. The facilitator serves as the primary assessor while other team members and parents sit away from the child and record observations and score portions of assessment tools relevant to their discipline. As the assessment progresses, team members may ask the facilitator to administer certain items relevant to the observer's discipline. Occasionally, an observer may assist the assessor or administer the items directly. Parents are present during the assessment to provide information, administer items if necessary, and validate the child's performance. (pp. 231-232)*

This form of assessment allows parents to play a range of roles. Wolery and Dyk (1984) found that parents generally preferred this model to the traditional model of individual assessments by each professional.

 IV. Some challenge questions

Handout 2-2 contains the Challenge Questions for this module. Use these questions as a way to summarize the points made and to prepare participants for small group decision-making.

How Will We Assess Family Resources, Priorities and Concerns?

THE PROVISIONS OF P. L. 99-457 related to assessing family resources, priorities and concerns represent one of the most challenging aspects of a family-centered approach. The broad goal for this session is to provide information for teams to develop a plan for identifying family resources, priorities and concerns. The specific goals are for participants to:

1. Develop a rationale for assessing family resources, priorities and concerns in early intervention.

2. Describe the major provisions of P. L. 99-457 regarding the assessment of family resources, priorities and concerns.

3. Recognize that families and family members will vary in the ways and extent to which they wish to have family resources, priorities and concerns assessed.

4. Identify a range of options for assessing family resources, priorities and concerns.

5. Identify and discuss issues likely to arise and choices that will need to be made in the process of family assessment.

Suggested Readings for the Facilitator
Bailey, D. B. (1991). Issues and perspectives on family assessment. *Infants and Young Children 4*(1), 26-34.

Bailey, D. B., & Blasco, P. M. (1990). Parents' perspectives on a written survey of family needs. *Journal of Early Intervention, 14,* 196-203.

Bailey, D. B., & Simeonsson, R. J. (1988). *Family assessment in early intervention.* Columbus, OH: Merrill Publishing Co.

Dunst, C. J., Trivette, C., & Deal, A. (1988). *Enabling and empowering families: Principles and guidelines for practice.* Cambridge, MA: Brookline Books.

Hanson, M. J., Lynch, E. W., & Wayman, K. I. (1990). Honoring the cultural diversity of families when gathering data. *Topics in Early Childhood Special Education, 10*(1), 112-131.

Trivette, C. M., Dunst, C. J., Deal, A. G., Hamer, A. W., & Propst, S. (1990). Assessing family strengths and family functioning style. *Topics in Early Childhood Special Education, 10*(1), 16-35.

Whitehead, L. C., Deiner, P. L., & Toccafondi, S. (1990). Family assessment: Parent and professional evaluation. *Topics in Early Childhood Special Education, 10*(1), 63-77.

Suggested Readings for Participants

Johnson, B. H., McGonigel, M. J., & Kaufmann, R. K. (1989; 1991). *Guidelines and recommended practices for the individualized family service plan.* Bethesda, MD: Association for the Care of Children's Health.

1989 Edition	*1991 Edition*
1. Chapter 4	1. Chapter 4
2. Chapter 5, pp. 37-39	2. Chapter 6
3. Appendix E	3. Appendix D

Suggested Outline of Session

A suggested outline for the session is presented in HANDOUT 3-1. Points for discussion and presentation are included here for each part of the outline. *DISCUSSION QUESTION: Before distributing the handout, ask participants to define family assessment; what do they think it means?*

I. P. L. 99-457 regulations on family assessment.

One reason we are so concerned about family assessment today is that P. L. 99-457 included it in the rules and regulations regarding the IFSP. The purpose of this section is to assure that participants are aware of what the law actually says. The five major points regarding family assessment are listed in the handout and displayed in TRANS-PARENCY 3-1. Inform participants that while P. L. 99-457 referred to assessing family needs and strengths, P. L. 102-119 changes this to assessing family resources, priorities and concerns.

 I.A. Designed to determine the resources, priorities and concerns of the family related to enhancing the development of the child

DISCUSSION QUESTION: What do you think this statement means? This question undoubtedly will generate a lot of discussion. One point that should be made if it does not surface is that this statement could be interpreted very narrowly (e. g., a focus on parent teaching skills), or very broadly (i. e., any aspect of family functioning may enhance the development of the child).

 I.B. Voluntary on the part of the family

This point is an important one to stress. Programs cannot establish family assessment procedures as part of their standard assessment battery. Families must be given the choice of whether to participate.

 I.C. Conducted by personnel trained to utilize appropriate methods and procedures

DISCUSSION QUESTION: Who do you think should be doing family assessments? Again, this will probably generate much discussion. The most likely suggestions will be social workers, family therapists, psychologists, or nurses. One point to make is that the interpretation of this guideline depends, in part, on one's definition of family assessment and the procedures used. *DISCUSSION QUESTION: Is it possible that some form of family assessment is every professional's responsibility?*

I.D. Based on information provided by the family through a personal interview

Although the regulations do not preclude the use of written surveys, observational tools, or other measures, the importance of face-to-face discussions with family members is emphasized. *DISCUSSION QUESTION: Why do you think this requirement was included in the regulations?*

 I.E. Incorporates the family's description of its resources, priorities and concerns related to enhancing the child's development

One view of family assessment is that it is a process by which professionals "evaluate" families. This guideline emphasizes the importance of the **family's** perception of resources, priorities and concerns rather than professional judgements.

 II. Some suggested definitions

A. *Family assessment.* A suggested definition for family assessment is included in the handout and displayed in TRANSPARENCY 3-2. Several points ought to be mentioned. First, it is an information-gathering process rather than a test. Second, that process has a particular purpose: to gather information in order to determine family priorities for goals and services. Of note is what is not included: family assessment is **not** an attempt to determine whether the family is a "good" or "competent" family, nor is it designed to compare families or family members with some ideal or norm group. *DISCUSSION QUESTION: Is this a definition that is acceptable to you? Ask for suggested revisions or an alternative definition.*

B. *Family needs.* A suggested definition for family needs is included in the handout and displayed in TRANSPARENCY 3-3. This definition views needs from the family's perspective; the focus is on needs for services, but goals are also viewed as needs. Some families may only identify child goals, but the identification of family priorities for children's needs should be viewed as one form of family assessment.

C. *Family resources.* The suggested definition for family resources (see handout and TRANSPARENCY 3-4) substitutes the word "resources" for "strengths" as stated in the regulations. Many have expressed the concern that use of the word "strengths" implies that some families are strong, whereas others are weak. Although this may be true, that is not the purpose of family assessment as we interpret it. Rather the purpose is to build on existing resources and identify additional resources needed to help achieve goals.

 III. Characteristics of effective family assessment

In addition to following the legal requirements for family assessment, several other factors ought to be considered as programs develop methods and procedures. Five such factors are listed on TRANSPARENCY 3-5.

 III.A. Conducted in a manner that is acceptable and positive for families

Although well-intentioned, the regulations regarding family assessment have the potential for alienating families if they perceive that process to be intrusive. It seems reasonable that the first criteria for evaluating the usefulness of any family assessment procedure is whether families view it as acceptable and positive. *DISCUSSION QUESTIONS: How or why might families view family assessment as intrusive or evaluative? Give some examples. What strategies might help increase the acceptability of assessments?* The assessment of parent-child interaction is one example of a "family" assessment that might be viewed as evaluative by some families, especially if they perceive the purpose of that assessment to be the determination of whether they are "good" parents.

III.B. Recognizes the importance of family styles, values and traditions

Families differ in many ways: structure, values, religious orientation, traditions, functions, communication styles, views of agencies, etc. Unfortunately, some family assessment procedures were developed from a framework that does not recognize or value this diversity. Ask participants to give examples of how families may value behaviors, skills, or other factors that many professionals may not perceive to be important. *DISCUSSION QUESTION: How can family assessments be designed to recognize variability in families?*

 ## III.C. Involves key family members

Family assessment usually turns out to be mother assessment. Yet research consistently suggests that fathers and mothers view their children in different ways and differ both in the number and types of needs expressed. In many families, other adults such as grandparents, aunts, or uncles may play key roles. Some families may want to involve siblings. *DISCUSSION QUESTION: What strategies could be useful in determining priorities of key family members other than the mother? Another question might be "Who are the key family members and how might that be determined?"*

 ## III.D. Uses "least intrusive and most natural strategies"

Formal assessments are likely to be the last procedure chosen in the family assessment arena. Often the most effective strategy will be informal conversations with family members in the context of regular routines, such as home visits, arrival and departure times, etc.

 ## III.E. Facilitates the identification of functional needs and resources

Ultimately the test of any family assessment procedure is whether it is functional: that is, does it facilitate the process by which professionals and families identify needs and resources?

IV. Some issues and considerations in family assessment

TRANSPARENCY 3-6 lists a number of issues that frequently arise in the discussion of family assessment.

IV.A. What strategies are useful for family assessment?

At least three broad strategies may be used in family assessments. Interviews and other discussions with family members constitute one strategy and may be the one used most frequently. The advantage to this procedure is that it is an interactive process allowing for the exploration of feelings and perceptions, as well as for empathetic responding. Four key skills needed for effective communication with family members (Winton, 1988) are listed and described in TRANS-PARENCY 3-7. The importance of effective communication as an assessment strategy cannot be overemphasized.

A second broad strategy is to use some form of written survey. Several practical measures have been developed in recent years. If you are using *Guidelines and Recommended Practices for the IFSP* as the text for this workshop, several such instruments are displayed. (Appendix E in 1989 edition or Appendix D in 1991 edition). If not, a sample measure (The Family Needs Survey) is available as HANDOUT 3-2. *DISCUSSION QUESTION: Ask participants to review one or more of the measures, noting similarity and differences between them.* The advantages of a survey include efficiency and the possibility that it may help families become aware of services that might be available to them. Disadvantages include its impersonal and some-times formal nature, inappropriateness for family members who cannot read, and lack of clarity about the meaning of some responses. Bailey and Simeonsson (1988) found that an open-ended question was essential to include, and Bailey et al. (1987) found that an interview following the survey was also important. Bailey and Blasco (1990) report a study of parent perceptions of one such instrument.

Other procedures may also be used for family assessments, but usually they would be used after some initial information was gathered through other procedures. One example would be an observation of parent-child interaction.

 ## IV.B. When should family assessments be done?

In some ways, family assessment begins with the first contact, since any interaction with a family is likely to provide information about family priorities for goals and services. Even the use of surveys early in the acquaintance process can sensitize professionals to a family's concerns and preferences, as well as let families know that the program is willing to assist in a variety of areas. A danger is that programs might artificially distinguish between child and family assessment when the assessment processes should be coordinated.

 ## IV.C. Will some families view family assessment as intrusive?

Of course the answer to this question is "yes." The study by Bailey and Blasco (1990), however, found that most parents were positive about the Family Needs Survey if it was presented as an option rather than a requirement for program participation. Remind participants that any family assessment must be voluntary, and discuss ways to ensure that families won't view the process as intrusive.

 ## IV.D. Whose job is family assessment?

This point was briefly addressed earlier, but still remains an issue. By this time, however, participants should be getting the message that family assessment, as defined here, is everyone's job. Ask them if they agree with this statement. *DISCUSSION QUESTION: If family assessment is everyone's job, what skills would be needed by **each** staff person in order to make this a reality?*

 ## IV.E. Should we ask about needs that we cannot help?

This question poses a constant dilemma for professionals trying to distribute limited time and resources to clients who sometimes seem to have unlimited needs. Family members also express frustration when they are asked to share information about needs for which the agency or professional has neither the intention nor the resources to provide assistance. Thus an important guideline is that professionals who ask about needs they are not willing to address are likely to create a sense of frustration on the part of some family members. On the other

hand, programs may want to reconsider traditional boundaries for professional practice and redefine what they mean by giving help. Full adoption of a family-centered philosophy of care pushes professionals and programs to extend traditional conceptions of what constitutes early intervention. Also, best practice with respect to help-giving does not mean that the helper does everything for the one helped. Appropriate help-giving practices seek to support clients in providing solutions to their own problems (Dunst, Trivette, & Deal, 1988). Assisting in discussing problems, identifying solutions, and securing resources are likely to be important supportive activities, thus providing some support for the determination of family needs that may not be directly solvable within a single agency or program. (Bailey, 1991)

 ## IV. F. What if I see a need that the family does not recognize?

This frequently asked question raised fundamental concerns regarding the role of professionals working with almost any family. If one accepts the definition offered earlier in this article, a need exists only if a family member expresses a desire for services to be obtained or outcomes to be achieved. Of course this does not mean that professionals should hide information or concerns from families. As a rule of thumb, however, this guideline is probably more defensible than overt or covert attempts to "force" families to recognize needs they do not perceive to exist. The likely consequence of such an approach is alienation and distrust.

A related question is "What if the family raises a concern that I don't think is very important?" The same basic premise should apply in this situation as well. It is well-known that one's perception of a stressor is often a greater determinant of stress than the event itself. Devaluing family concerns as insignificant creates an imbalance in the parent-professional relationship and will likely serve as a barrier to future collaborative work. (Bailey, 1991)

 ## IV.G. When is an assessment of family resources appropriate?

Although the assessment of family strengths was designed to emphasize positive aspects of families, attempts to assess strengths could be viewed as value-laden. *DISCUSSION QUESTION: What are some examples of family strengths?* Usually this question will generate suggestions such as "good communication" or "equal decision-making". For most, however, you can make the point that not all families would agree with that, and in fact would resent being evaluated from that perspective. An alternative might be to focus instead on **resources** and to assess resource availability in the context of identified needs. This point is emphasized in P. L. 102-119, which officially changes the word "strengths" to "resources".

 ## V. Review the challenge questions for this module (HANDOUT 3-3)

How Will We Involve Families in Team Meetings and Decision-making?

THE TEAM MEETING represents another opportunity for examining practices to emphasize a family-centered approach. The primary goal for this session is to provide information to assist teams in developing and implementing a plan for allowing and assisting families to be involved in the team meeting and decision-making process. The specific goals are for participants to:

1. Know components of P. L. 99-457 rules and regulations regarding the interdisciplinary team.

2. Develop a rationale for involving families in the team meeting and decision-making process.

3. Recognize that families and professionals will vary in the ways and extent to which they wish to be involved in team meetings and decision-making.

4. Describe dimensions of effective teams and the dynamics of team interaction, including decision-making, communication, and conflict resolution.

5. Identify a range of options for supporting families who wish to be involved in team meetings and decision-making.

Suggested Readings for the Facilitator

Bailey, D. B. (1984). A triaxial model of the interdisciplinary team and group process. *Exceptional Children, 51,* 17-25.

Kilgo, J. L., Richard, N., & Noonan, M. J. (1989). Teaming for the future: Integrating transition planning with early intervention services for young children with special needs and their families. *Infants and Young Children, 2*(2), 37-48.

McGonigel, M. J., & Garland, C. W. (1988). The individualized family service plan and the early intervention team: Team and family issues and recommended practices. *Infants and Young Children, 1*(1), 10-21.

Nash, J. K. (1990). Public Law 99-457: Facilitating family participation on the multidisciplinary team. *Journal of Early Intervention, 14,* 318-326.

Spencer, P. E., & Coye, R. W. (1988). Project BRIDGE: A team approach to decision-making for early services. *Infants and Young Children, 1*(1), 82-92.

Suggested Readings for Participants

Johnson, B. H., McGonigel, M. J., & Kaufmann, R. K. (1989; 1991). *Guidelines and recommended practices for the individualized family service plan.* Bethesda, MD: Association for the Care of Children's Health.

1989 Edition	*1991 Edition*
1. Chapter 4, pp. 28-30	1. Chapter 4, pp. 35-38

Suggested Outline of Session

A suggested outline for the session is presented in HANDOUT 4-1. The following notes are related to each major heading in the handout.

 I. Rationale for Teams

DISCUSSION QUESTION: Why do we have teams in early intervention? Of course one reason is that the law mandates a multidisciplinary perspective on services. But the rationale for teams extends beyond the mandate. Participants will likely be able to generate many of the reasons why teams exist. Be sure that at least the following points get made:

1. The complex nature of many disabilities requires high levels of specialization in multiple areas.

2. Our knowledge base is rapidly increasing, and no one person or discipline is likely to have all of the answers.

3. Need to integrate information and services.

 ## II. P. L. 99-457 regulations regarding teams and team meetings

The regulations include several key pieces of information relevant to the composition of teams and required activities.

 ## II.A. Defines multidisciplinary

The definition of "multidisciplinary" found in the regulations is displayed in TRANSPARENCY 4-1. As is evident, multidisciplinary means the involvement of two or more disciplines or professions. No other number is specified, nor is a core of essential disciplines described. The regulations do list an array of early intervention services, as displayed in TRANSPARENCY 4-2, any of which could have representatives on the team.

 ## II.B. Describes who must be present at the IFSP meeting.

The regulations state that each initial and annual IFSP meeting must include each of the participants listed in TRANSPARENCY 4-3. Review each of these, and ask participants if their meetings currently adhere to these guidelines. Of course some issues are left unresolved. For example, if the service needs have yet to be identified, how can relevant service providers be known?

 ## II.C. Describes other conditions regarding IFSP meetings.

Other regulations regarding IFSP meetings are displayed in TRANS-PARENCY 4-4. These include requirements regarding timelines, review processes, etc. Several *DISCUSSION QUESTIONS* are likely to arise here or should be raised: *(1) How can both child and family needs be assessed in 45 days?* [Be sure to mention here the possibility of an interim IFSP] *(2) Infants change so rapidly. Does a one year IFSP really make sense? (3) To what extreme must we take "settings and*

times convenient to the family?" (4) Do you think most families would prefer to have the meeting at home or at your office? [An interesting activity here is to ask participants to describe unusual places they have held team meetings. Be sure that the point gets made that different families will have different preferences].

 ## III. Why is it difficult for families to feel a part of a team?

There have been a number of research studies that have documented that parents often do not participate in IEP meetings to any great extent, and that many professionals believe that a passive role is appropriate for parents. Why is this the case? Several reasons why families may find it difficult to feel they are a part of a team are listed in TRANSPARENCY 4-5. These should be reviewed and discussed. Throughout, ask participants to give examples of problems they have seen.

 ## III.A. Professionals often discount parent perspectives or priorities.

One reason is that professionals sometimes do not value parent perspectives or priorities. Hopefully, if the issues and guidelines discussed in the previous three modules are followed, this will not be a problem in early intervention programs. Realistically, however, participants will probably be able to provide several examples of this problem.

 ## III.B. Professionals often see the child only from their own discipline's perspective.

Professionals from various disciplines may assign a discipline-specific label to a child or focus only on their discipline's treatment strategies. If parents see professionals engaging only in "parallel play" with each other rather than cooperating to look at the child as a whole, they may feel that this is not really a team activity.

III.C. Parents often enter poorly functioning groups.

It takes time and skill for a group to become effective. Bailey (1984) describes many common problems of teams, including those associated with lack of experience together as a group, subsystem problems (e. g., a dominant team member or two factions within a group), or whole team problems (e. g., disorganization, lack of purpose). The intent of the regulations is that each family may have a uniquely constituted team. This is important for individualization, but will create some difficulties since groups will have difficulty maturing together as teams.

 III.D. Parents often are not involved in the initial planning stages.

In the old school model of IEP meetings, parents are brought in after professionals have done all of their work. By involving families in the assessment process, participation is likely to be enhanced.

 III.E. Parents are not given meaningful roles on the team.

Of course, the role of the family must be different from the role of professionals, since they are the recipient of services. Each professional, however, usually has a well-defined role in the meeting, whereas parents do not.

 III.F. Parents often are not prepared for the meeting or supported in their participation.

The research of Turnbull and others shows that preparing parents prior to the meeting and engaging in supportive behaviors during the meeting is likely to enhance their participation.

 III.G. A group of professionals can be very intimidating.

No matter how nice professionals are, a group can be very intimidating. This may be especially true for parents of young children with disabilities who have never had to experience a team meeting for their child before. Of course it can be an especially intimidating experience for parents who for reasons of race, poverty, education, or skill are very different from the group of professionals on the team.

 IV. Strategies for facilitating family involvement in team meetings and decision-making

Several strategies for enhancing family involvement are listed in HANDOUT 4-1.

 IV.A. Offer choices for involvement.

Families (and family members) will vary in the ways they want to participate in the team process. Providing choices about these activities is one way to build a family-centered approach.

 IV.B. Focus the assessment process and the team meeting on parents' concerns.

Some team meetings we have witnessed have focused on the child without regard to the concerns expressed by families. A model in which family questions and concerns provides the initial basis for the team meeting is likely to make families feel more a part of the team and more invested in the process.

 IV.C. Involve families in child assessment to the extent they want to be involved.

By allowing and encouraging families to be involved in the child assessment process, family priorities are identified early and families feel they have something to share in the meeting. Professionals have their scores and test results, whereas parents bring only their experiences. These experiences, however, are essential to a true understanding of the child and his or her needs. A study by Brinckerhoff and Vincent (1986) demonstrates the importance of this point. In the study, they had parents complete a description of home routines and a developmental inventory. They also met with a professional who discussed the IEP process with them and gave examples of how the information they provided could fit into the team meeting. The authors found that these activities increased family contributions to team meetings and decision-making. More goals were generated by the parents, greater team agreement was noted, and more home-based activities were generated.

 IV.D. Conduct individual preconference meetings with families to help prepare them for the experience.

This is especially important prior to the first team meeting for a family.

 IV.E. Ensure good communication skills on the part of all team members.

The communication skills described in the family assessment module (displayed in TRANSPARENCY 3-7) should be shown again to the group. The point should be made that these skills are not just useful for family assessment; a study by Bailey et al. (1988) found that professionals who received training in communication skills reported that the training helped them in communicating with other professionals as well. Each of the four skills described is essential for effective participation in group meetings. You might want to focus here on various questioning skills, particular on the way that questions can be used to help encourage parents to generate ideas for goals and services. Winton (1988) describes the circular questioning strategy as important in this context.

 IV.F. Organize meetings in ways to maximize parent involvement.

Bailey (1989a) describes the following strategy for organizing a meeting:

> *Another procedure for increasing the potential for parental involvement is to organize the meeting according to skill areas and discuss First areas of high importance to families, such as self-help or motor skills. In each area, the parents are asked to describe how they perceive their child's skills and needs in the area being considered, such as toileting or feeding. An open-ended question, such as "Could you tell us about how Dani eats at home now?" is used to initiate the discussion. If necessary, professionals can prompt parents for additional or more precise information through use of specific closed-ended questions such as "Does she pick up a spoon on her own?" Once parents have provided detailed information about the skill being discussed, professionals supplement that information from their own*

assessments. Any discrepancies in perception of ability are discussed, and then parents are asked to identify priorities for intervention within that skill domain. Professionals attend to and reinforce those priorities whenever possible by establishing goals related to each. If additional goals are deemed important by professionals, they are then mentioned and discussed. This process sends a clear message to parents that they are important members of the decision-making team and that their perspectives and priorities for their children are valued by professionals seeking to provide the most appropriate early intervention services possible. (p.12)

IV.G. Agree on team goals and philosophy.

If team members have different perspectives on their roles or on the goals of the team, those differences may sometimes be reflected in the team meeting. Of course different perspectives are essential; otherwise, there would be no need for a team. But there ought to be agreement among all team members on such key issues as a commitment to family support. Hopefully the activities in Module 1 will help teams recognize the need for a coherent philosophy.

IV.H. Develop a structure or plan for decision-making.

Team meetings should be flexible enough to accommodate a wide variety of needs and styles. Research has shown, however, that groups that agree on the process by which decisions will be made are more effective than those who do not.

IV.I. Learn to disagree effectively.

Two things can happen related to disagreements that make teams ineffective. One is when disagreement becomes the underlying theme of every discussion. The other is when team members become so familiar with each other's thinking that they no longer feel a need to discuss an issue; they simply make a decision and move ahead. Research on groups has shown that effective disagreement, defined as the discussion of alternative perspectives on needs, goals, or services, is essential to good decision-making.

SECTION III:
Appendices

Guidelines for Leading Case Study Discussions

Guidelines for Leading Case Study Discussions

1. Know the Case in Detail

It is important for the instructor to read the case well in advance of the training and remember it in detail. The instructor should not have to rely on notes or the case itself during group discussion.

2. Use Questions to Guide the Discussion

Questions are the main means of guiding trainees through the process of problem-solving (i. e., application of principles to the case). Questions, however, should not be of the type that aim to lead trainees in the direction of a "right" answer. For the most part, questions should be open-ended. They should serve to challenge the trainees to examine their thinking processes in sorting out the details of the case and considering possible outcomes of their decisions.

3. Don't Fish for Pat Answers

Care must be taken not to imply to trainees that you already know the solution to the case and that you are trying to get them to come up with the answer you have in mind. If this occurs, the trainees will stop using their own thinking processes to arrive at a course of action. Instead, they will spend their time trying to figure out how you are thinking and what you want them to say. Again, the focus will be on the solution rather than the process of arriving at the solution.

4. Maintain a Nonjudgmental Stance

Maintaining a nonjudgmental stance throughout case discussion is easier said than done. It is extremely important, however, that participants be able to join in the discussion and state their opinions without fear of even the most subtle hint of criticism from the instructor. It does indeed take practice to lead the discussion through questions without implying any disapproval of participants' contributions.

5. Let Trainees Carry the Discussion

It is quite tempting to move the discussion along at a faster rate or to prematurely summarize participants' contributions and "solve" the case. But, please don't. If the discussion is moving along, don't get involved. Even when the discussion gets bogged down or there is a conflict among participants, don't feel obliged to get involved right away. It is better to hold back just a little and see if they can work it out by themselves. If they can't, then you have the responsibility to get the discussion back on track through questioning, summarization, or redirection,

6. Redirect If the Discussion Drifts into Generalizations

Quite often discussion of a case will drift off into generalizations about "all parents", "all families", or "all children". The discussion may also drift in the direction of participants providing extreme examples of the type of situation that is given in the case in order to support their positions such as "What if the family in this case did (e. g., a more extreme action)?" or "What if the child had (e. g., a more extreme disability)?" When this occurs, the instructor should redirect the discussion away from the theoretical and back to the particular situation of the case under discussion.

7. Encourage Alternative Solutions and Ideas

Good problem-solving or decision-making involves the generation of multiple solutions or courses of action and deciding among the options. Oftentimes, discussion of a case will head off in one direction without consideration of alternative perspectives or solutions. If the direction taken represents good application of the principles, skills, or knowledge provided in training, the instructor is tempted to allow this to happen. It is a good policy, however, to encourage alternative ideas and solutions even when good application skills are being demonstrated. If not, the implication may be that the instructor "approves" of the direction the discussion is taking and participants with other perspectives will not voice them. Playing the devil's advocate is sometimes an effective way of getting alternative opinions out on the table.

8. Draw Attention to Neglected Facts or Unverified Assumptions

Participants may at times make assumptions about the case which are not based upon the actual facts presented. Such assumptions should be pointed out to the group before the discussion proceeds too far along. Likewise, participants may ignore some information in the case in the discussion. This too should be pointed out through questioning or insertion on the part of the instructor.

9. Play Out the Case When a Solution is Offered

When a course of action is suggested by participants, it is often instructive to ask what the possible outcomes of following through with the suggested solution might be. Another strategy is to play out the family's reaction to the course of action yourself. This may be done by accepting the course of action and making up a story about one or more ways that the family may respond (family behavior or dialogue). Then ask the trainees whether this was the response they had in mind and what they would do next. Playing out the case serves to point out the dynamic nature of the interactions between families and professionals and the need to consider the possible outcomes of their decisions.

10. Assist Trainees in Communicating

Sometimes trainees have a difficult time putting into words what they want to say. They may become frustrated with themselves or with other members of the group if they are misunderstood. If this occurs, restating the trainee's ideas in an acceptable manner may relieve frustration and keep the trainee active in the discussion. Use this strategy sparingly.

11. Summarize the Discussion Periodically

A lot can be said in a short period of time when a number of participants are involved in the discussion. The trainees may lose sight of the direction the discussion is or should be taking. An important role of the instructor is to pull together or summarize what has been said and provide some new objectives for the discussion. This may be done at several points in the discussion and especially if the discussion becomes rambling. For example, the instructor may summarize all of the options that have been suggested and start the discussion in the direction of selecting among the alternatives (i. e., analyzing the pros and cons of each option).

12. Relate the Discussion Back to the Training Content

At several points during the discussion, but especially at the end of the discussion, the instructor should relate the case and its discussion back to the material covered in training. This may be done in a short monologue by the instructor at the close of the case discussion. But it is sometimes more instructive to assist trainees in relating the case discussion back to the training material through questioning.

Family Orientation of Community & Agency Services (FOCAS)

FOCAS:
Family Orientation of Community and Agency Services

Don Bailey, Ph.D.

Frank Porter Graham Child Development Center
University of North Carolina at Chapel Hill

Name or ID Number: ___/___/___/___
(please put the last four digits of your Social Security number)

Date: ___/___/___
MM DD YY

Directions: The purpose of this scale is to determine your perceptions of how families are included in your early intervention program or community. The scale consists of 12 items addressing various program components. Each item can be scored from 1 to 9. In rating each item, first read all of the descriptors. On the scale above the descriptors, circle the number that best represents your program or community's typical inclusion of families in the context of early intervention. Then, on the scale below the descriptors, circle the number that represents where you would like for your program or community to be on this dimension. Use the even-numbers if your program or community falls between the descriptors specified under the odd-numbered ratings.

This scale was developed as part of the Carolina Institute for Research on Infant Personnel Preparation, an early childhood research institute funded by the Special Education Program of the Office of Special Education and Rehabilitative Services, U.S. Department of Education (Grant #G0087C3064). The author expresses appreciation to Rune Simeonsson, Robin McWilliam, Shirley Geissinger, Gail Huntington, Pam Winton, Patti Blasco, Sharon Palsha and P. J. Cushing for their suggestions and contributions. Persons interested in using the scale may copy and distribute it for training or evaluation purposes, so long as its source is recognized. The institute would welcome feedback regarding its usefulness and would appreciate a copy of any reports or data summaries based on an application of the instrument. Address all correspondence to Don Bailey, Ph.D, Frank Porter Graham Child Development Center, Campus Box# 8180, UNC-CH, Chapel Hill, NC, 27599.

A. PROGRAM PHILOSOPHY ABOUT WORKING WITH FAMILIES

Where are you now?

1	2	3	4	5	6	7	8	9
I don't believe our program has an expressed philosophy of early intervention.		Our program has a general philosophy of early intervention but it does not include a specific family focus.		Our program is now in the process of considering and discussing a philosophy regarding a family focus in early intervention.		Our program has a well-articulated philosophy which includes a family focus in early intervention.		A family focus is central to our program philosophy.

Where do you want to be?

1	2	3	4	5	6	7	8	9

B. FAMILY-PROFESSIONAL COLLABORATION IN DEVELOPING A PROGRAM PHILOSOPHY

Where are you now?

1	2	3	4	5	6	7	8	9
Neither parents nor professionals have worked together to develop a program philosophy.		Some staff have worked together to develop a program philosophy.		All professionals on the team have been actively involved in developing a program philosophy.		Our program has worked collaboratively with family members to develop a program philosophy.		Parents and professionals regularly and collaboratively evaluate our program philosophy and make changes or modifications when needed.

Where do you want to be?

1	2	3	4	5	6	7	8	9

Where are you now?

1	2	3	4	5	6	7	8	9
Professionals make all decisions about who is to assess and what is to be assessed, with little information provided for parents.		Professionals take time, before any assessments are conducted, to explain to parents what assessments they are going to do and the rationale for each.		Professionals present an assessment plan and ask parents for feedback.		Professionals work together with parents to form an assessment plan.		Professionals provide decision-making opportunities for parents who want to coordinate child assessments.

Where do you want to be?

1	2	3	4	5	6	7	8	9

Where are you now?

1	2	3	4	5	6	7	8	9
Professionals conduct all child assessments, relying primarily on direct testing or observational strategies.		Professionals ask parents to provide information about their child's behavior or development.		Professionals seek to understand the child's behavior and development in the context of family routines, perceptions, values, and priorities.		Professionals provide opportunities and assistance for parents who want to participate in the process of assessing their children.		Professionals provide encouragement and support for parents who would like to have a major role in conducting child assessments.

Where do you want to be?

1	2	3	4	5	6	7	8	9

(over) ☞

E. IDENTIFYING FAMILY NEEDS AND STRENGTHS/RESOURCES

Where are you now?

1	2	3	4	5	6	7	8	9

We don't currently gather information about family needs or resources.

Professionals occasionally gather information from a parent about family needs. This information is likely to focus on child-care or teaching activities and is not a part of our regular assessment process.

Professionals regularly gather information about family needs. This information usually comes from one parent and focuses primarily on family needs related to child care or development.

Professionals regularly gather information about family needs and resources. Usually, this information comes from one family member and may address family needs not specific to the child with handicaps or who is at risk.

Professionals are willing to gather information about the needs and resources of both immediate and extended family members. This may include a broad array of needs, ranging from child care to financial needs, community services, or family functioning.

Where do you want to be?

1	2	3	4	5	6	7	8	9

F. FAMILY PARTICIPATION IN DECISIONS ABOUT IDENTIFYING FAMILY NEEDS AND RESOURCES

Where are you now?

1	2	3	4	5	6	7	8	9

Professionals make all decisions about who is to assess and what needs/resources are to be assessed, with little information or choice for parents.

Professionals take time, before any family assessments are conducted, to explain to parents what assessments they are going to do and the rationale for each.

Professionals present a family assessment plan and ask parents for feedback.

Professionals work together with parents to form a family assessment plan.

Professionals provide families with a range of choices, including whether needs and resources are assessed, how that information will be shared, and priorities for services based on those needs.

Where do you want to be?

1	2	3	4	5	6	7	8	9

G. PARENT PARTICIPATION IN TEAM MEETINGS

Where are you now? 1 2 3 4 5 6 7 8 9

1–2	3–4	5–6	7–8	9
Parents attending the IEP/IFSP meeting are assigned a passive role. Few efforts are made to secure their input.	Parents participate to the extent that they take the initiative.	Parents are "given their turn" to contribute in team meetings.	Parents are encouraged and supported in taking an equal role with professionals in the team meeting.	Professionals provide encouragement and support for parents who would like to lead the team meeting.

Where do you want to be? 1 2 3 4 5 6 7 8 9

H. PARENT ROLES IN DECISION-MAKING

Where are you now? 1 2 3 4 5 6 7 8 9

1–2	3–4	5–6	7–8	9
Professionals write the IEP/IFSP and present it as a final document to parents for their signatures.	Professionals present a plan for goals and services to parents and provide opportunities for feedback.	Professionals give parents an opportunity to make suggestions for goals and services prior to writing the IEP/IFSP.	Professionals and parents work as equal partners in developing the IEP/IFSP.	Professionals provide support and encouragement for parents who would like to assume a leadership role in making decisions about goals and services.

Where do you want to be? 1 2 3 4 5 6 7 8 9

(over)

I. IFSP FORMAT

Where are you now?

1	2	3	4	5	6	7	8	9
We currently do not have an IFSP format and have not developed a plan for deciding on one.		We have plans for an IFSP format but have not yet implemented it.		We have implemented an IFSP format, but it is only marginally successful.		We have an IFSP format that professionals have found to be workable and effective.		We have an IFSP format that parents have endorsed as workable and effective.

Where do you want to be?

1	2	3	4	5	6	7	8	9

J. FAMILY GOALS ON THE IEP/IFSP

Where are you now?

1	2	3	4	5	6	7	8	9
We currently do not include family goals on the IEP/IFSP.		We are considering including family goals on the IEP/IFSP, but have not yet done so.		If the family wishes, we will write family goals in certain, well-defined areas.		Some flexibility in family goals, based on family priorities.		Highly flexible goals that may, if desired by parents, include siblings and extended family members and may address a wide array of child or family needs.

Where do you want to be?

1	2	3	4	5	6	7	8	9

K. FLOW OF SERVICES

Where are you now?

1	2	3	4	5	6	7	8	9
Programs in our community do not work together at all in providing early intervention services. We do not have a local Interagency Coordinating Council.		Our community is beginning to explore ways for agencies to collaborate.		Our community is beginning to implement collaborative and integrated services.		Programs in our community generally work together in providing early intervention services.		Our community has a well-integrated, flexible, and cooperative system of early intervention services. Parents may enter the system in a variety of ways and can feel assured of equal access to services.

Where do you want to be?

1	2	3	4	5	6	7	8	9

L. CASE MANAGEMENT

Where are you now?

1	2	3	4	5	6	7	8	9
We currently do not have a case management system and have not developed a plan for one.		We have plans for a case management system but have not yet implemented it.		We have a case management system, but it is only marginally successful.		We have an effective and active case management system.		Professionals provide support and encouragement for parents who would like to assume some case management responsibilities.

Where do you want to be?

1	2	3	4	5	6	7	8	9

Appendix C
Documenting Participant Satisfaction

Participant Evaluation of Workshop

We are very interested in your reactions to the activities of this workshop. Please take a few minutes to respond to the following questions.

1. Did the workshop address topics that are important for your program?

1	2	3	4	5
Not at all		Somewhat		A Lot

Comments:

2. Was the format helpful in establishing concrete goals for change?

1	2	3	4	5
Not at all		Somewhat		A Lot

Comments:

3. Did you feel that the decision-making process was truly a group effort?

1	2	3	4	5
Not at all		Somewhat		A Lot

Comments:

4. Is it likely that the goals established will be achieved?

1	2	3	4	5
Not at all		Somewhat		A Lot

Comments:

please turn to back ☞

5. What were the most positive aspects of the workshop for you?

6. What changes would you suggest in the workshop?
   Format Changes—

   Content Changes—

7. Are there any other comments you would like to share about the workshop?

Thank you for your cooperation.

Appendix D
Master Copies of Handouts

Overview and Program Philosophy

I. Why have a workshop on becoming family-centered?
A. P.L. 99-457: legislative foundations for a family-centered approach in early intervention
B. Changing ideas about what it means to be family-centered
C. The IFSP is but one indication of a family focus ideally, a family-centered approach should permeate all facets of early intervention
D. Research and experience suggest that changing early intervention services to include a focus on families is a challenging and difficult task
E. How can this change be accomplished?

II. What are some Key Questions or areas of decision-making for teams?
A. Developing or revising program philosophy to reflect a family-centered approach
B. Involving families in child assessment
C. Assessing family resources, priorities and concerns
D. Involving families in team meetings and decision-making
E. Deciding on IFSP goals and formats
F. Implementing the IFSP and providing case management
G. Other

III. How will the workshop be organized?
A. Three components: information, case application, team decision-making
B. Emphasis on team planning
  1. Where are you?
  2. Where do you want to be?
  3 How will you get there?
  4. Who is responsible for what?
  5. How will you monitor your progress?
C. Some comments on the change process

IV. What is our philosophy about working with families?
A. Why have a program philosophy?
B. What is a family-centered philosophy?
C. Some examples of philosophy statements or principles
D. A summary of some assumptions
  1. Family-centered
  2. Ecologically-based
  3. Individualized
  4. Culturally sensitive
  5. Enabling and empowering
  6. Needs-based
  7. Coordinated with other community agencies
  8. Normalized
  9. Collaborative

E. Some issues in developing a program philosophy
    1. Philosophy vs. policies vs. regulations
    2. Individual beliefs vs. program philosophy
    3. Who establishes the philosophy in your program?
    4. Involving families in philosophy development
    5. Applying the philosophy in daily interactions between all staff and families
    6. Communicating a program's philosophy
F. Some challenge questions

References

Bailey, D. B. (1987). Collaborative goal setting with families: Resolving differences in values and priorities for services. *Topics in Early Childhood Special Education, 7*(2), 59-71.

Bernheimer, L. P., Gallimore, R., & Weisner, T. S. (1990). Ecocultural theory as a context for the Individual Family Service Plan. *Journal of Early Intervention, 14,* 219-233.

Brewer, E. J., McPherson, M., Magrab, P. R., & Hutchins, V. L. (1989). Family-centered, community-based, coordinated care for children with special health care needs. *Pediatrics, 83,* 1055-1060.

Dunst, C. J., Trivette, C., & Deal, A. (1988). *Enabling and empowering families: Principles and guidelines for practice.* Cambridge, MA: Brookline Books.

Espe-Sherwindt, M., & Kerlin, S. L. (1990). Early intervention with parents with mental retardation: Do we empower or impair? *Infants and Young Children, 2*(4), 21-28.

Policy Statements or Principles That Address the Relationship Between Programs and Families

FEDERAL REGISTER, JUNE 22, 1989, P. 26309:

Part H recognizes the unique and critical role that families play in the development of infants and toddlers . . . It is clear, both from the statute and the legislative history of the Act, that the Congress intended for families to play an active, collaborative role in the planning and provision of early intervention services. Thus these regulations should have a positive impact on the family, because they streng-then the authority and encourage the increased participation of parents in meeting the early intervention needs of their children.

DUNST, 1985, P.170:

The goal of early intervention is to empower families to make informed decisions and take control over their lives.

BREWER, McPHERSON, MARGRAB & HUTCHINS, 1989, P. 1055:

Family-centered care is the focus of philosophy of care in which the pivotal role of the family is recognized and respected in the lives of children with special health needs. Within this philosophy is the idea that families should be supported in the natural care-giving and decision-making roles by building on their unique strengths as people and families. In this philosophy, patterns of living at home and in the community are promoted; parents and professionals are seen as equals in a partnership committed to the development of optimal quality in the delivery of all levels of health care. To achieve this, elements of family-centered care and community-based care must be carefully interwoven into a full and effective coordination of the care of all children with special health needs.

ELEMENTS OF FAMILY-CENTERED CARE

1. Recognition that the family is the constant in the child's life while the service systems and personnel within those systems fluctuate.
2. Facilitation of parent/professional collaboration at all levels of health care:
   • care of an individual child;
   • program development, implementation and evaluation; &
   • policy formation
3. Sharing of unbiased and complete information with parents about their child's care on an ongoing basis in an appropriate and supportive manner.
4. Implementation of appropriate policies and programs that are comprehensive and provide emotional and financial support to meet the needs of families.
5. Recognition of family strengths and individuality and respect for different methods of coping.
6. Understanding and incorporating the developmental needs of infants, children, and adolescents and their families into health care delivery systems.
7. Encouragement and facilitation of parent-to-parent support.
8. Assurance that the design of health care delivery systems is flexible, accessible, and responsive to family needs.

-Shelton, Jeppson, & Johnson, 1987,
Family-centered care for children with special health care needs.

PRINCIPLES UNDERLYING THE IFSP PROCESS

- Infants and toddlers are uniquely dependent on their families for their survival and nurturance. This dependence necessitates a family-centered approach to early intervention.

- States and programs should define "family" in a way that reflects the diversity of family patterns and structures.

- Each family has its own structure, roles, values, beliefs, and coping styles. Respect for and acceptance of this diversity is a cornerstone of family-centered early intervention.

- Early intervention systems and strategies must reflect a respect for the racial, ethnic, and cultural diversity of families.

- Respect for family, autonomy, independence, and decision making means that families must be able to choose the level and nature of early intervention's involvement in their life.

- Family/professional collaboration and partnerships are the keys to family-centered early intervention and to successful implementation of the IFSP process.

- An enabling approach to working with families requires that professionals re-examine their traditional roles and practices and develop new practices when necessary—practices that promote mutual respect and partnerships.

- Early intervention services should be flexible, accessible, and responsive to family needs.

- Early intervention services should be provided according to the normalization principle—that is, families should have access to services provided in as normal a fashion and environment as is possible and that promote the integration of the child and family within the community.

- No one agency or discipline can meet the diverse and complex needs of infants and toddlers with special needs and their families therefore, a team approach to planning and implementing the IFSP is necessary.

-Johnson, McGonigel & Kaufman, 1989

What is our philosophy about working with families?

	Issues to Consider	Is Change Needed?	Rank Order	Type of Change Needed	Resources/ Activities
1.	Is a family focus central to our program philosophy and shared by all team members?	__ Yes __ No			
2.	Have families been invited to collaborate in the development of our program philosophy?	__ Yes __ No			
3.	Are our interactions with families positive?	__ Yes __ No			
4.	Do we respect family diversity in beliefs, values, and coping styles?	__ Yes __ No			
5.	Are our services flexible enough to meet individual family needs?	__ Yes __ No			
6.	Does our IFSP process recognize and support informal support systems?	__ Yes __ No			
7.	Do we allow families to refuse help?	__ Yes __ No			
8.	Other:	__ Yes __ No			

Involving Families in Child Assessment

I. P.L. 99-457 regulations related to child assessment
A. Must be "comprehensive" and multidisciplinary
B. Differentiates evaluation and assessment
C. Must be conducted by trained personnel
D. Must include
1. Review of health and medical records
2. Levels of functioning in
a. Cognitive
b. Physical
c. Communication
d. Social or Emotional
e. Adaptive
3. Statement of unique needs of child
E. Must include both needs and strengths
F. Assessments must be "family-directed"
G. 45-day timeline
H Nondiscriminatory, informed consent, confidentiality

II. Rationale for family involvement in child assessment
A. Characteristics of traditional assessment processes
B. Problems/limitations with traditional assessment
C. Goals of child assessment:
1. To determine eligibility for services
2. To identify functional intervention goals
3. To identify children's strengths and unique behavioral styles
4. To reinforce parents' feelings of competence and worth
5. To build a shared and integrated perspective on child and family needs and resources
6. To create a shared commitment to intervention goals

III. Strategies for involving parents in child assessment
A. Determining family goals for assessment process
B. Determining family preferences for involvement
C. Some parent & other caregiver roles and strategies for each
1. **Receiver** of information gathered by professional
2. **Observer** of professional assessment
3. **Informant** about behavior and development
4. **Describer** of perceived skills/competencies
5. **Interpreter** of child's strengths and needs
6. **Participant** in gathering data

IV. Issues in family involvement in child assessment: case study examples

References

Bailey, D. B. & Wolery, M. (1989). *Assessing infants and preschoolers with handicaps.* Columbus, OH: Charles E. Merrill Publishing Co.

Bloch, J. S. & Seitz, M. (1989). Parents as assessors of children: A collaborative approach to helping. *Social Work in Education,* 226-244.

Brinkerhoff, J. L. & Vincent, L. J. (1986). Increasing parental decision-making at the individualized educational program meeting. *Journal of the Division for Early Childhood, 11,* 46-58.

Garwood, S. G. & Sheehan, R. (1989). *Designing a comprehensive early intervention system: The challenge of Public Law 99-457.* Austin TX: Pro-Ed.

Healy, A., Keesee, P. D. & Smith, B. S. (1989). *Early services for children with special needs: Transactions for family support.* (second edition). Baltimore: Paul H. Brookes.

Kjerland, L. & Kovach, J. (1990). Family-staff collaboration for tailored infant assessment. In E.D. Gibbs & D.M. Teti (Eds.), *Interdisciplinary assessment of infants* (pp. 287-298). Baltimore: Paul H. Brookes.

How will we involve families in child assessment?

Issues to Consider	Is Change Needed?	Rank Order	Type of Change Needed	Resources/ Activities
1. Are we complying with all P.L. 99-457 regulations regarding child assessment?	___ Yes ___ No			
2. Do we try to determine family preferences about the purpose and format of child assessment, as well as their wish to be involved?	___ Yes ___ No			
3. Do we convey assessment information in a sensitive and jargon-free fashion?	___ Yes ___ No			
4. Does the family's perception of child needs determine the focus of child assessment?	___ Yes ___ No			
5. Do we listen to family's preferences in determining settings, times, and parent roles in child assessment?	___ Yes ___ No			
6. Do we address children's strengths in the assessment process?	___ Yes ___ No			

Assessing Family Resources, Priorites and Concerns

I. P.L. 99-457 regulations on family assessment
A. Designed to determine the resources, priorities and concerns of the family related to enhancing the development of the child
B. Voluntary on the part of the family
C. Conducted by personnel trained to utilize appropriate methods and procedures
D. Based on information provided by the family through a personal interview
E. Incorporates the family's description of its resources, priorities and concerns related to enhancing the child's development.

II. Some suggested definitions
A. **Family Assessment:** The process by which professionals gather information in order to determine family priorities for goals and services, as well as resources available to meet those priorities.
B. **Family Need:** A family's expressed desire for services to be obtained or outcomes to be achieved
C. **Family Resources:** The support systems a family has or needs in order to meet expressed needs or achieve designated outcomes.

III. Characteristics of effective family assessment
A. Conducted in a manner that is acceptable and positive for families
B. Recognizes the importance of family values, styles, and traditions
C. Involves key family members
D. Uses "least intrusive and most natural" strategies
E. Facilitates the identification of functional needs and resources

IV. Some issues and considerations in family assessment
A. What strategies are useful for family assessment?
    1. Interviews and informal discussions
    2. Survey instruments and rating scales
    3. Other procedures
B. When should family assessments be done?
C. Will some families view family assessment as intrusive?
D. Whose job is family assessment?
E. Should we ask about needs that we cannot help?
F. What if I see a need that the family does not recognize?
G. When is an assessment of family resources appropriate?

References

Bailey, D. B. (1991). Issues and perspectives in family assessment. *Infants and Young Children.,* *4*(1), 26-34.

Bailey, D. B. & Blasco, P. (1990). Parents' perceptions of a written survey of family needs. *Journal of Early Intervention, 14,* 196-203.

Bailey, D. B. & Simeonsson, R. J. (1988). Assessing needs of families with handicapped infants. *Journal of Special Education, 22,* 117-127.

Bailey, D. B., & Simeonsson, R. J. (1988). *Family assessment in early intervention.* Columbus, OH: Charles E. Merrill Publishing Co.

Dunst, C., Trivette, C. M. & Deal, A. G. (1988). *Enabling and empowering families: Principles and guidelines for practice.* Cambridge, MA: Brookline Books.

Winton, P. J. (1988). Effective communication between parents and professionals. In D. Bailey & R. Simeonsson (Eds.), *Family assessment in early intervention* (pp. 207-228). Columbus, OH: Charles E. Merrill Publishing Co.

Winton, P. J. (1988). The family-focused interview: An assessment measure and goal-setting mechanism. In D. Bailey & R. Simeonsson (Eds.), *Family assessment in early intervention* (pp 185-206). Columbus, OH: Charles E. Merrill Publishing Co.

Family Needs Survey
(Revised, 1990b)

Child's Name:_____ Person Completing Survey:_____

Date Completed:____/____/____ Relationship to Child: _____

Dear Parent:

Many families of young children have needs for information or support. If you wish, our staff are very willing to discuss these needs with you and work with you to identify resources that might be helpful.

Listed below are some needs commonly expressed by families. It would be helpful to us if you would check in the columns on the right any topics you would like to discuss. At the end there is a place for you to describe other topics not included in the list.

If you choose to complete this form, the information you provide will be kept confidential. If you would prefer not to complete the survey at this time, you may keep it for your records.

Would you like to discuss this topic with a staff person from our program?

TOPICS	No	Not Sure	Yes
Information			
1. How children grow and develop			
2. How to play or talk with my child			
3. How to teach my child			
4. How to handle my child's behavior			
5. Information about any condition or disability my child might have			
6. Information about services that are presently available for my child			
7. Information about the services my child might receive in the future			
Family & Social Support			
1. Talking with someone in my family about concerns			
2. Having friends to talk to			
3. Finding more time for myself			
4. Helping my spouse accept any condition our child might have			
5. Helping our family discuss problems and reach solutions			
6. Helping our family support each other during difficult times			
7. Deciding who will do household chores, child care, and other family tasks			
8. Deciding on and doing family recreational activities			
Financial			
1. Paying for expenses such as food, housing, medical care, clothing, or transportation			
2. Getting any special equipment my child needs			
3. Paying for therapy, day care, or other services my child needs			
4. Counseling or help in getting a job			
5. Paying for babysitting or respite care			
6. Paying for toys that my child needs			

TOPICS	Would you like to discuss this topic with a staff person from our program?		
	No	Not Sure	Yes
Explaining to Others			
1. Explaining my child's condition to my parents or my spouse's parents			
2. Explaining my child's condition to his or her siblings			
3. Knowing how to respond when friends, neighbors, or strangers ask questions about my child			
4. Explaining my child's condition to other children			
5. Finding reading material about other families who have a child like mine			
Child Care			
1. Locating babysitters or respite care providers who are willing and able to care for my child.			
2. Locating a day care program or preschool for my child			
3. Getting appropriate care for my child in a church or synagogue during religious services			
Professional Support			
1. Meeting with a minister, priest, or rabbi			
2. Meeting with a counselor (psychologist, social worker, psychiatrist)			
3. More time to talk to my child's teacher or therapist			
Community Services			
1. Meeting & talking with other parents who have a child like mine			
2. Locating a doctor who understands me and my child's needs			
3. Locating a dentist who will see my child			

Other: Please list other topics or provide any other information that you feel would be helpful to discuss.

_____

_____

Is there a particular person with whom you would prefer to meet?

_____

_____

Thank you for your time.
We hope this form will be helpful to you in identifying the services that you feel are important.

The Family Needs Survey was developed by Don Bailey, Ph.D. and Rune Simeonsson, Ph.D.
For further information, write the authors at the Frank Porter Graham Child Development Center,
CB#8180, University of North Carolina, Chapel Hill, NC 27599

How will we identify family resources, priorities and concerns?

	Issues to Consider	Is Change Needed?	Rank Order	Type of Change Needed	Resources/ Activities
1.	Are we complying with all P.L. 99-457 regulations regarding family assessment?	__ Yes __ No			
2.	Do parents know that we are responsive to family priorities and concerns?	__ Yes __ No			
3.	Do we try to determine family preferences regarding family assessment?	__ Yes __ No			
4.	Have we agreed on a flexible model & alternative procedures for assessing family resources, priorities and concerns?	__ Yes __ No			
5.	Is family assessment recognized as part of each team member's role?	__ Yes __ No			
6.	Does each team member have the skills needed to communicate effectively with families?	__ Yes __ No			
7.	Other:	__ Yes __ No			

Family Involvement in the Team Meeting and Decision-making

I. Rationale for teams
A. Complex nature of many disabilities requires high levels of specialization
B. Increasing knowledge base and a recognition that no one person or discipline has all of the answers
C. Need to integrate information
D. Need to integrate services

II. P. L. 99-457 regulations regarding teams and team meetings
A. Defines "multidisciplinary" as the involvement of two or more disciplines or professions in the provision of integrated and coordinated services
B. States that the IFSP must be based on a multidisciplinary evaluation and describes who must be present at the IFSP meeting:
   1. Parent(s)
   2. Other family members as requested by parents
   3. Advocate or person outside of family, if requested
   4. Service coordinator
   5. Persons involved in conducting evaluations and assessments
   6. Persons who will be providing services
C. Describes other conditions regarding the IFSP meeting
   1. Within 45 days of referral
   2. IFSP must be reviewed every 6 months or more frequently if warranted or requested
   3. Annual evaluation and revision
   4. Settings and times convenient to families
   5. Native language or other mode of communication

III. Why is it difficult for families to feel like they are really a part of a team?
A. Professionals often discount parent perspectives or priorities
B. Professionals often see the child only from their discipline's perspective
C. Parents often enter poorly functioning groups
D. Parents often are not involved in the initial planning stages
E. Parents are not given legitimate/meaningful roles on the team
F. Parents often are not prepared for the meeting or supported in their involvement in meetings
G. A group of professionals can be very intimidating, intentional or not

IV. Strategies for facilitating family involvement in team meetings and decision-making

A. Offer choices for involvement from the beginning
B. Focus the assessment process and the team meeting on parents' concerns
C. Involve families in child assessment to the extent they want to be involved
D. Conduct individual preconference meetings with families to help prepare them for the experience
E. Ensure good communication skills on the part of all team members
F. Organize meetings in ways to maximize parent involvement
G. Agree on team goals and philosophy
H. Develop a structure or plan for decision-making
I. Learn to disagree effectively
J. Support the development of each team member
K. Ensure effective leadership

References

Bailey, D. B. (1984). A triaxial model of the interdisciplinary team and group process. *Exceptional Children, 51,* 17-25.

Brinkerhoff, J. L. & Vincent, L. J. (1986). Increasing parental decision-making at the individualized education program meeting. *Journal of the Division for Early Childhood, 11,* 46-58.

Kilgo, J. L., Richard, N. & Noonan, M. J. (1989). Teaming for the future: Integrating transition planning with early intervention services for young children with special needs and their families. *Infants and Young Children, 2* (2), 37-48.

McGonigel, M. J. & Garland, C. W. (1988). The individualized family service plan and the early intervention team: Team and family issues and recommended practices. *Infants and Young Children, 1* (1), 10-21.

Nash, J.K. (1990). Public Law 99-457: Facilitating-family participation on the multidisciplinary team. *Journal of Early Intervention, 14,* 318-326.

How will we involve families in team meetings and decision-making?

ID# __/__/__
(Last 4 digits of SS#)

	Issues to Consider	Is Change Needed?	Rank Order	Type of Change Needed	Resources/ Activities
1.	Are we complying with all P. L. 99-457 regulations regarding the team and family participation on it?	__ Yes __ No			
2.	Do we try to determine family preferences regarding their role on the team?	__ Yes __ No			
3.	Do families determine team membership?	__ Yes __ No			
4.	Do we employ strategies to make sure that families feel comfortable participating in team meetings?	__ Yes __ No			
5.	Do we function as a team or as individual specialists?	__ Yes __ No			
6.	Do we hold our meetings in settings and times convenient to the family?	__ Yes __ No			
7.	Do we respect parents' decisions even if professionals disagree?	__ Yes __ No			
8.	Other:	__ Yes __ No			

 # How Will We Write the IFSP?

I. Mandated components of the IFSP
    A. Child's present level of development
    B. Family resources, priorities and concerns
    C. Major child and family outcomes
    D. Criteria, timeline and procedures for determining progress
    E. Services to be provided
    F. Date and duration of services
    G. Name of service coordinator
    H. Transition procedure

II. Some issues in developing the IFSP
    A. The IFSP as an integrative tool
    B. The functional role of the IFSP
    C. Desired features of the IFSP form
    D. Semantic issues: objectives, goals, outcomes, projects
    E. Ensuring accountability
    F. Writing "higher order" goals
    G. Legal issues

References

Bailey, D. B. & Simeonsson, R. J. (1988). *Family assessment in early intervention.* Columbus, OH: Charles E. Merrill Publishing Co.

Bailey, D. B., Winton, P. J., Rouse, L. & Turnbull, A. P. (1990). Family goals in infant intervention: Analysis and issues. *Journal of Early Intervention, 14,* 15-26.

Dunst, C. J., Trivette, C. & Deal, A. (1988). *Enabling and empowering families: Principles and guidelines for practice.* Cambridge, MA: Brookline.

Garwood, S. G. & Sheehan, R. (1989). *Designing a comprehensive early intervention system.* Austin, TX: Pro-Ed.

McGonigel, M. J & Garland, C. W. (1988). The Individualized Family Service Plan and the early intervention team: Team and family issues and recommended practices. *Infants and Young Children, 1* (1), 10-21.

ID# __/__/__/__
(Last 4 digits of SS#)

What will be the format of an IFSP or IED?

Issues to Consider	Is Change Needed?	Rank Order	Type of Change Needed	Resources/ Activities
1. Are we complying with all P.L. 99-457 regulations regarding the IFSP or IEP document?	___ Yes ___ No			
2. Do we try to determine family preferences regarding their role in developing or writing the plan?	___ Yes ___ No			
3. Have we agreed on a format that will work for us?	___ Yes ___ No			
4. Do we write goals using words that are acceptable and understandable for families?	___ Yes ___ No			

Characteristics of Effective Family Assessment

- Conducted in a manner that is acceptable and positive for families

- Recognizes the importance of family values, styles and traditions

- Involves key family members

- Uses least intrusive and most natural strategies

- Facilitates the identification of functional needs and resources

Issues in Family Assessment

- What strategies to use?

- When should family assessments be done?

- Will families view family assessment as intrusive?

- Whose job is family assessment?

- Should we ask about needs we cannot help?

- What if I see a need the family does not recognize?

- When is an assessment of resources appropriate?

Skills for Communicating Effectively with Families

Listening Skills

Focusing and following what a family member has to say using verbal and nonverbal listening skills

Reflecting Feelings

The ability to accurately and sensitively identify and reflect a family member's feelings

Reflecting Content

The ability to restate the content of a family member's message briefly and concisely by paraphrasing and summarizing

Effective Questioning

Structuring questions in a way that promotes understanding of the family (assessment) and decision making (goal setting)

P.L. 99-457 Definition of Multidisciplinary

Multidisciplinary means
   the involvement of two or more
   disciplines or professions in the
   provision of integrated and coordinated
   services, including evaluation,
   assessment, and development of the
   IFSP.

P. L. 99-457 Listing of Early Intervention Services

Audiology

Service Coordination

Health

Medical

Nursing

Nutrition

Occupational Therapy

Physical Therapy

Psychology

Social Work

Special Instruction

Speech/Language Pathology

Transportation

IFSP Participants

P. L. 99-457 States That Each Initial & Annual IFSP Meeting Must Include the Following:

- Parent or Parents

- Other Family Members

- Advocate

- Service Coordinator

- Evaluators/Assessors

- Service Providers

P. L. 99-457 Regulations Regarding IFSP Meetings

- Within 45 days of referral

- Review at least every six months

- Annual evaluation

- Settings & times convenient to family

- Native language

- Sufficient advance notice

- Arrange for participation of persons who cannot attend

Factors That Make it Difficult for Families to Feel Part of a Team

- Professionals discount parent perspectives or priorities

- Professionals see child from single discipline's perspective

- Parents are not involved in planning stages

- Parents are not given meaningful roles

- Parents are not prepared for the meeting or supported in their involvement

- A group of professionals can be very intimidating

IFSP Elements 1-7

③ Child & Family Goals	④ Services	⑤ Timelines/ Outcome Criteria	⑥ Coordinated Management	⑦ Transition Plan

Child & Family Assessment

① Child Needs:

Child Characteristics:

② Family Needs:

Family Characteristics:

What Functions Would You Like the IFSP to Serve?

Some Functions of the IFSP

- Archival

- Planning

- Communicative

- Integrative

- Monitoring

- Evaluation

What Practical Features Would You Like in an IFSP Form?

Components of a Good Behavioral Objective

- **Who** will change or do the behavior

- A statement of the specific **behavior** to be performed

- A description of the **conditions** under which the behavior is expected

- **Criteria** for determining whether the objective has been accomplished

(From Dunst, Trivette, & Deal, 1988)

EVALUATION RATING SCALE

Ratings	Criteria
N A	No longer a need, goal, aspiration or project
1	Unresolved or worse; unattainable
2	Unchanged; still a need, goal, aspiration or project
3	Resolved or attained; but not to the family's satisfaction
4	Unresolved or partially attained, but improved
5	Resolved or attained to the family's satisfaction

Date	Notes/Comments

Five Levels of Goal Attainment (Head Start)

Level 1
No effort at achieving the goal

Level 2
Initial effort toward achieving goal

Level 3
Some progress toward goal; more effort needed for success

Level 4
Goal partially achieved; success expected

Level 5
Goal achieved

How Do the Regulations for P. L. 99-457 Define Service Coordination?

The activities carried out by a service coordinator to assist and enable a child eligible under this part and the child's family to receive the rights, procedural safeguards, and services that are authorized to be provided under the State's early intervention program.

Specific Service Coordination Activities

1. Coordinating the performance of evaluation and assessments

2. Facilitating and participating in the development, review, and evaluation of IFSPs

3. Assisting families in identifying available service providers

4. Coordinating and monitoring the delivery of available services

5. Informing families of the availability of advocacy services

6. Coordinating with medical and health providers

7. Facilitating the development of a transition plan to preschool services

Assignment & Qualifications of
Service Coordinators

- From the profession most immediately relevant to the child's or family's needs

- Qualifications—
  must have demonstrated knowledge about:
  1. Infant & toddlers who are eligible under this part
  2. Part H of the Act & the regulations
  3. The nature & scope of services available under the State's early intervention program, the system of payments for services in the State, and other pertinent information

- If the states have existing service coordination systems, may use or adapt

- Comments state that the intent of Congress was for service coordination responsibilities be assigned to "an appropriate, qualified public agency employee." However, parents apparently now can be service coordinators.

Some Alternative Labels for Service Coordinator

Expediter
Continuity Agent
Case Manager
Broker
Ombudsman
Patient Representative
Advocate
Systems Agent
Helper
Partner
Synthesizer
Human Development Liaison Specialist

The Ecology of Service Coordination

A. The value of service coordination

1. By professionals & programs
2. Administrative value
3. Service coordinator's own sense of value
4. Clients' value

B. Administrative support & placement

1. Allocation of time & resources
2. Relationships within & between systems
3. Elimination of multiple service coordination systems

C. Authority or clout

1. Legal
2. Administrative
3. Clinical
4. Fiscal